FAMINE IN THE LAND OF ULSTER

The Irish Potato Blight of the Mid-Nineteenth Century

Michael Sheane

ARTHUR H. STOCKWELL LTD
Torrs Park   Ilfracombe   Devon
Established 1898
www.ahstockwell.co.u

British Library Cataloguing-in-Publication Data.
A catalogue record for this book is available
from the British Library.

Arthur H. Stockwell Ltd bears no responsibility
for the accuracy of events recorded in this book.

By the same author:
Ulster & Its Future After the Troubles (1977)
Ulster & The German Solution (1978)
Ulster & The British Connection (1979)
Ulster & The Lords of the North (1980)
Ulster & The Middle Ages (1982)
Ulster & Saint Patrick (1984)
The Twilight Pagans (1990)
Enemy of England (1991)
The Great Siege (2002)
Ulster in the Age of Saint Comgall of Bangor (2004)
Ulster Blood (2005)
King William's Victory (2006)
Ulster Stock (2007)

ISBN 978-0-7223-3897-1
Printed in Great Britain by
Arthur H. Stockwell Ltd
Torrs Park   Ilfracombe
Devon

Contents

Foreword

The Irish famine lasted from 1845 to 1852, and it is essential to our understanding of the development of modern Ireland. It affected the whole of Ireland, but it developed regional variations. Today a realistic assessment has taken place. The consequences of the famine were most severe in the west and south of the island, but other parts of the country were also greatly affected, including Belfast, where it interfered with commercial progress.

Over 150 years has passed since this horrific event, and there has been renewed historical interest in what one writer has called 'The Great Hunger'. New information has been published at a steady rate, and the full range of documentary evidence which has survived from the period had been little researched until recently. However, the effects of the Great Hunger in Ulster have been mostly ignored. The belief has arisen that there was no famine in Ulster, but its impact must have varied from district to district, and from county to county. The economy of Ireland was undergoing change, and in parts of rural Ulster this helped to dampen the effects of the famine. Industry became established in a number of key towns. There was much poverty in Ulster, and this was mirrored in the south and west of Ireland. Although several relief measures were introduced by the government, most of the relief was inadequate. The consequences of the famine were distress, disease, eviction and a lot of mortality. All this was evident throughout Ulster, where death rates were the highest in the island, although there were also high death rates in Connaught and Munster. The folk memory of the Great Hunger has remained strong in the province.

Before the Great Hunger the Irish economy had gone through a series of changes which were to the benefit of small tenants and cottiers. Most notably, in Ulster there was a decline in the domestic linen industry, caused by the rise in new technology. The textile industry, especially linen, was becoming centred on Belfast and other towns in Ulster. Incomes fell and smallholders and small freeholders were denied access to other sources of revenue. In County Londonderry the decline of domestic industry had contributed to an increase in migration from the county in pre-famine times. This was also a characteristic of other counties, namely Armagh, Cavan and Monaghan.

In County Armagh the impact of technological change was to make itself felt in the vulnerability of weavers, at the same time as the decline of rural Ulster. People had to manage as best they could. The transformation that took place in linen production coincides with attempts by landlords and their agents to modernize their estates. A precondition of this transformation was that the subdivisions should be recorded and revised. Consolidation of holdings was evident throughout Ulster, even before the famine, but it was accelerated during the mid-nineteenth century, facilitated by death, emigration, eviction and the voluntary surrender of land.

Paddy Duffy's study of County Monaghan concentrates on change that took place in the rural landscape and society. There was considerable overcrowding within County Monaghan since land had become fragmented and towns subdivided. This had come about by the expansion of the linen industry in the eighteenth century. The possession of a loom made smallholdings more viable. By 1841 the decline in the linen industry left large numbers of people without any income. In the years before the Great Hunger many of the poor existed on the verge of destitution. They had often to seek assistance, usually in the form of rent rebates, blankets or food. Large estates such as the Shirley estate in County Monaghan provided this form of intermittent welfare. The introduction of the Poor Law in 1838 led to a decline in private clients.

The process of industrialization took place in the countryside and the leading towns in Ireland. The Act of Union of 1800 had brought about a decline in trade between England and Ireland. Belfast also benefited from colonial trade. In Belfast there were regions, such as Smithfield, which remained vulnerable. Paupers were commonplace and people were employed to drive them off the streets.

Where the population was struggling there was pre-famine rural poverty in the north and west of Ireland. At the start of the nineteenth century, County Armagh was the most densely populated of the nine counties. The competition for land brought about a growth in sectarian violence.

6

There was also rural poverty in other parts of Ulster. For example, Paddy Duffy records that on the eve of the famine there were 400 people per square mile in parts of County Monaghan – a density of population similar to that in the west of Ireland. There was great dependence upon the potato amongst the rural poor of the province, not the 'lumpe' variety, which was common throughout the rest of Ireland, but 'cups', 'doe blacks', 'red downs' and 'black seddings'. In County Cavan there was also a dearth of adequate housing, as well as an increased reliance upon the potato. Near Lurgan the poor ate potatoes for breakfast, dinner and supper. Thus, during a period of decline in the countryside, industry started to bloom, but economic vulnerability and extreme destitution were on the rampage.

Before the advent of the Great Hunger, there had been trouble on the land. Between 1800 and 1850 it is estimated that there were eight subsistence crises and three famines in the island. Food shortages could be an indication of the vulnerability of the Irish economy. Cahal Dallat believed that the administrative and fund-raising activities which occupied the local gentry in committees (for example, 1817 and 1831) proved invaluable during the hunger. Private soup kitchens were set up in County Antrim in 1847. The machinery of government supported local efforts and these had become well established, and had already been extended by 1845. In County Londonderry a study showed that upon the first appearance of the potato blight in the country the traditional mechanisms of welfare swung into action, supported by the clergy, landlords and large farmers – all providing sustenance for the destitute.

The 1840s famine was characterized by its longevity. The potatoes rotted in the fields, and reports first appeared in the Irish newspapers on 6 September 1845. The same blight had been reported in Belgium, France, Germany, England, the Netherlands during the summer of 1845 and America in 1844. Ireland was unique for its high depopulation as a result of the famine. The potato was the staple food of two fifths of the population, but the spread of the famine in Europe after 1845 provided a ready market for Irish grain, providing useful income during the famine years.

One of the first manifestations of the blight occurred at Florence Court in County Fermanagh. Here the Royal Irish Constabulary reported that whole fields were destroyed. There were sightings of the disease in County Londonderry even earlier. In 1845 the damage done by the famine was not consistent throughout the Ulster countryside. In County Antrim the blight destroyed the potatoes in Antrim town, Ballycastle, Ballymoney and Lisburn. At Larne, however, much of the crop was

7

eatable. In County Down turnips were destroyed by the same blight that hit the potatoes.

By October 1845 many boards of guardians – the local relief officials – started to consider other types of food for the inmates of the workhouses. Rice, oats, bread or soup started to replace the potato. The first year of the potato famine was managed by the local relief facilities, which had been established throughout Ulster, so there was little call to draw upon government assistance. In County Cavan, in the spring of 1846, there existed many cases of extreme suffering. A large portion of the population was close to starvation.

In 1846 the potato blight had returned to Ireland, and was more widespread than in the previous years. Sightings were made as early as July. A Dublin newspaper recorded in September 1846 that the disease had already destroyed the crop in the counties of Antrim, Londonderry, Tyrone, Armagh and Monaghan. There were only two exceptions – Cave Hill in Belfast and the neighbourhood of Glenarm. The local hostels were no longer able to serve potatoes, and rice was provided instead. A more extensive blight occurred in 1846 and marks the peak of the severity of the Great Hunger.

In June 1846 Robert Peel's Tory government fell from power. The Whigs, or Liberals, now took over, led by Lord John Russell. He modified the relief measures of the previous year, but the new measures were costly and ineffective. One James Grant demonstrated that even in County Tyrone, one of the counties least affected, the public works administration was unable to deal with the demands made upon it. A meeting was held in East Omagh on 13 October 1846 to introduce public works. It took a further two months before the procedure had been completed. An initial grant of money was made, but another month went by before the procedure could be effected. Grant pointed out the procedure to be adopted in regard to establishing drainage, for bad drainage was a factor in propagating the disease. By the time that relief came about, many of the Gaels were suffering from fever, dysentery and diarrhoea. Wages were low in the public works and it was difficult to support a family, so added pressure was put on the local relief committees. At Clogher the relief committees gave supplementary relief to those working in the public works by providing cut-price food for them.

The role of the relief committees was very important. The government insisted that food could not be sold below the market value, but this measure was not liked and was ignored by some members of the committee. In County Tyrone this policy was opposed by the Moy and Dunnamanagh committees. James Grant saw the situation deteriorate

8

at the end of 1846, and a more flexible approach was made.

The potato crop had now failed for the second time, but the horrors of the famine were confined to the west of the country. Trevor McCavery showed that by the beginning of 1847 there was great suffering in parts of County Down. The same situation obtained at Skibbereen in County Cork. This situation was disliked by a number of local landlords and gentry who prided themselves on living in the most economically successful part of the county. McCavery's detailed study of the Newtownards Union was passed by London. The failure of the potato in 1846 coincided with a decline in the linen industry: this substantially reduced the incomes of many hand-loom weavers. The Newtownards Union helped the destitute by the setting-up of a public works committee, the establishment of relief committees, increased pressure for admission to the local workhouse, and the establishment of soup kitchens. These measures were also adopted in other parts of the country. In Newtownards, and in the neighbouring union, the relief measures were provided without the financial assistance of the government. This avoided the necessity for repayment at a later date, but poverty was still rampant. McCavery gives a description of people queuing at soup kitchens at Newtownards. They were half famished, and many were without sufficient clothes.

Suffering was seen in other parts of Ulster too. The Lurgan Union, centre of one of the most industrialized parts of the province, also experienced great destitution. In the first week of February there was a fall in mortality in the Lurgan workhouse, but it was highest in Ulster in the same week. The Lurgan workhouse was closed for further admissions. A member of the Society of Friends, visiting the union in April 1847, said that the situation was akin to that in County Cork. The greater part of the famine relief was provided through local workhouses.

The Poor Law system, which had been operating in England since the sixteenth century, was introduced into Ireland in 1838. As a consequence of this Act, Ireland was divided into 130 unions (collections of townlands). Each union had its own workhouse and elected board of guardians. The 1838 law bypassed county boundaries and some unions had portions in two, three or, occasionally, four counties. Workhouses varied in size, ranging from the Cavan workhouse, which held 1,200 paupers, to the Armagh, Belfast and Downpatrick workhouses, each built to hold 1,000 paupers. The Castlederg and Gortin workhouses could hold 200 inmates each.

The conditions in workhouses played a secondary role in relief from the Great Hunger. Following the second failure of the potato crop in

1846, pressure was put on the workhouses through Ireland (including Ulster). By the end of 1848, twenty-one out of the forty-three workhouses in the province were full to capacity, so additional buildings were erected. Demand for workhouse relief varied from union to union. At Magherafelt in County Londonderry it was estimated that there was a forty-three per cent increase in the number of sick, especially those suffering from dysentery and fever, and therefore there was a rise in mortality.

In 1846, during Christmas week, twenty-three inmates of the Omagh workhouse, including sixteen children, met their deaths. By February 1847 the situation had deteriorated further, so the boards of commissioners ordered that the workhouse should not increase its admissions. The workhouse remained closed until July 1847.

There were many children under the age of fifteen in the workhouses, and this was a feature of the whole of Ireland. It was further pointed out that the number of paupers was highest in Ulster. By 1848 children made up half the population of the workhouses.

In some cases the need to provide shelter brought the guardians into conflict with the central board of commissioners. The Cookstown guardians requested food for the destitute, for they were unable to provide workhouse relief. Their request was refused. At the Lowtherstown board of guardians in County Fermanagh there was open conflict and paid officials were appointed. Their workhouses were perhaps the best administered in the county. The Armagh Union was regarded by the Poor Law Commissioners as the best administered in Ireland. The Lurgan Union, however, was beset by poor management. Gerard MacAtasney pointed out that in the two years from May 1845 to May 1847 the workhouse had seven different masters. During this period many of the guardians showed little interest in the workhouse. The doctor was incompetent, the workhouse was insanitary and disease-ridden, and the diet was inadequate.

Working in the workhouse could be dangerous for relief officers, and two of them died of fever. Father Gallogly observed that fever was no respecter of social status. In Cavan it killed more rich people than poor. There was great fear of disease, and it could lead to actions of great inhumanity: the temporary fever hospital at Belturbet, County Cavan, was burnt down in April 1847. In County Donegal, from as early as November 1846, the workhouse stopped admitting the poor. A member of the Society of Friends who visited the workhouse in 1846 described it as in bad condition. Administration was insufficient and poor times had a bad effect on the guardians' ability to provide relief. Mortality rates were high in the workhouse and there was a lack of clothes. The winter of 1846/7 was very cold, with snow falling in Donegal as late as April 1847. The master of the workhouse reported that during the snowy weather the poor were working out of doors without shoes or leggings. Religious devotions were also analysed. It was concluded that the influx of Protestants into the workhouse could be measured by the number of books and Bibles that were supplied throughout 1847. These items were purchased when the inmates who died in the workhouse were being buried coffin-less in mass graves due to lack of funds.

The Temporary Relief Act of February 1847 provided for the establishment of government soup kitchens through Ireland and this was probably the most useful measure that the British Government took during the famine. By July 1847 over three million souls were receiving free daily rations of food. There were regional variations: in parts of the west of Ireland, as in Gort, Swindon and Westport, over eighty per cent of the local inhabitants depended upon relief in the summer of 1847. In the unions of Belfast and Newtownards no soup kitchens were opened. Belfast was engaged in raising funds for other parts of the country. They were pleased that they did not need financial assistance from the government.

A need of fresh accommodation for the sick came to light after the autumn of 1847, when the Poor Law was held responsible for relieving the famine. However, a number of unions still needed financial assistance from the government. Twenty-two unions were declared to be in urgent need. The majority of these were in the south and west of Ireland. The Glenties Union, in County Donegal, was placed in this category.

There was relatively little potato blight in 1847. Only a small crop had been sown.

There was also a slump in the British economy in 1846–7 and this had repercussions in Belfast and its hinterland, especially in the linen industry. In County Armagh it was observed that the general recession left the local weavers without resources. Many of them were already destitute. In Belfast many workers were now unemployed or were placed on a lower wage. This put great pressure on the workhouses. In 1848 over one million people throughout Ireland were on Poor Law relief.

Sometimes the bedrooms in the workhouses became the scene of ideological battles regarding the nature of destitution and how it should be dealt with. In the Newtownards Union, for example, it was discovered that the majority of the guardians voted not to give outdoor relief following the passage of the Poor Law Amendment Act in 1847, which made it legal for the first time. William Sharman Crawford, the chairman, resigned and said that the ruling was unjust, uncharitable and unchristian. McCavery identifies that the real victims of the decision were those who could not receive relief until they were near starvation. The Poor Law had been increased by a rise in taxation during the famine and contributed to the number of Ulster unions. John Cunningham, who examined the impact of the potato blight in County Fermanagh, observed that by May 1847 the Enniskillen Union was £5,000 in debt. Later the Enniskillen guardians were dismissed and their successors were paid officials appointed by the central commissioners. They found the financial difficulties of the union no less intractable in Cavan, Cootehill, Enniskillen, and Lowtherstown, two of which are in County Fermanagh. The dismissal of the Lowtherstown Union was not popular and resulted in a Parliamentary inquiry into the case.

A commission was set up in 1848 to recommend the creation of new workhouses. Thirty-three unions raised funds, making a total of 163. Most of the new unions were in the south and west of Ireland. Here blight had been as extreme as in 1846. Only two were chosen for Ulster: they were the Bawnboy Union, which had been created from parts of Enniskillen, and the Cavan Union. The Killybegs and Kilrea unions were created out of Coleraine and Magherafelt unions.

There was a considerable amount of distress in parts of Ireland after 1848, resulting in a further change of policy by the government. In May 1849 the Rate-in-Aid tax was introduced, and this affected the Irish Poor Law Unions.

Some areas of Ulster were beginning to emerge from the worst effects of the famine, but in a number of unions the poor were still beset by hunger, homelessness, disease and exhaustion. Father Gallogly's study of Cavan demonstrates that deaths from the fever were higher in 1849 than they had been in 1847, and that workhouse deaths were higher in 1849 than at any time during the Great Hunger. The Bishop of Kilmore was alarmed and he called for relief committees to be re-established in the region.

The Rate-in-Aid tax was unpopular with boards of guardians in Ulster, who claimed they were financially penalized. The Ulster guardians started a campaign in which they opposed the new policy. Diverse terms were used. The impact of the potato famine in the south and west was compared with that of the north of Ireland (Ulster). One John Cunningham recorded that at Lisnaskea, in County Fermanagh, the boards of guardians protested that the Rate-in-Aid tax was being imposed upon the peaceful and industrious people who lived in Ulster.

There was support for the lazy, and there was an indolent population in the south and west of Ireland. Gerard MacAtasney recorded the proceedings of a meeting held in Lurgan during May 1849, which said that the suffering of the people in County Armagh had matched the worst scenes in the west of Ireland.

The landlords of Ulster came under stern criticism, but recent research has shown that their bark was worse than their bite. Elsewhere Jim Donnelly has suggested that the response of the landlords was to thoroughly work their estates with modern techniques. This was the case especially in relation to evictions. After 1847 there were added incentives to evict impoverished smallholders as the tax burden on landlords increased greatly. The land was cleared with a view to good management. The consequences were evictions and land consolidation. There were fewer evictions in County Londonderry than in other parts of Ireland; but there is widespread evidence of landlords helping their tenants to emigrate. Land was cleared and made ready for fresh tenants. The agent of the London Companies (landowners in the county) advised that there was immediate opportunity to develop/plant part of the land. Lord Londonderry's agent in County Down said that his object was to press those who were destitute into emigration.

Neighbouring landlords had their own views. In County Down, for example, Trevor McCavery identified the reactions of the landlords, William Sharman Crawford and Lord Londonderry. William Sharman Crawford responded to the news of the famine by reducing rents and promising further assistance to his tenants. Lord Londonderry, however, resisted this action because a rent reduction would result in inconvenience for others. Lord Londonderry also found himself at the centre of a public controversy when a newspaper criticized him and his wife for donating only £30 to famine relief. The newspaper claimed that he had been corrupt. Both Lord Londonderry and his agent laid great emphasis upon donations. McCavery also noted that in 1848 Lord Londonderry made extensive repairs to his mansion at Mount Stewart, and also to Holdernesse House, his London residence. Cahal Dallat described Lady Londonderry's building of Garron Tower in County Antrim.

The general consensus was that where the landlords resided on their estates the local population was not put in jeopardy. The involvement of local landlords in relief committees seems to have been largely beneficial. At Ballinderry Glebe in County Londonderry, a clergyman complained that a consequence of absenteeism was that the local relief committees were left without funds and the poor remained in an abject condition. The Society of Friends noted the indifference of the landlords. They visited Ireland in the winter of 1846/7. Gerard MacAtasney quoted the Reverend Clements of County Armagh as blaming the famine at Tartaraghan on the evils of absenteeism. James Grant, however, pointed out that the worst resident landlords were only concerned with their own estates, and had virtually no interest beyond that. This was partly due to financial reasons, as most of the burden for funding famine-relief schemes fell on the local landlords. The areas at greatest risk appeared to be those where there were many different landlords. The land was subdivided and was therefore liable to higher taxation. If the landlords were absentees, they took little interest in their Irish estates.

The activities of merchants and professionals during the famine were not very well recorded. These groups were sometimes active on local relief committees and as guardians of the local workhouses. Their behaviour was not to be recommended. Father Gallogly described how the food shortages during the famine were exploited by merchants and businessmen in Cavan as an opportunity for profiteering. Instances were recorded of retailers holding back supplies of corn in order to create scarcity. There was also the practice of charging exorbitant prices for food.

Clergymen of all denominations during the famine behaved well. This was the case in Ulster and in Ireland as a whole. Within Ulster, Church of Ireland, Catholic and Presbyterian ministers worked together on relief committees that dealt with famine matters, or what they called 'God's visitation'. They helped to raise funds in money or in kind. The local gentry's conscience had been pricked.

There was also an important dialogue between the local providers of relief and officials in Dublin or in London.

It is hard to say exactly when the famine ceased in Ulster. After 1848 the potato blight started to disappear from most areas in Ireland, but there were still isolated pockets, mainly in the south-west of the country. In Ulster there was an end to recession and a return to good harvests. However, the blight had not altogether disappeared from Ulster. Cahal Dallat pointed out that it reappeared in County Antrim as late as 1852. Emigration, evictions, disease and death were still higher than pre-famine levels.

Ireland had been thoroughly stricken by the famine. Between 1845 and 1851 at least one million Irish people died from starvation or famine-related disease. A further one million emigrated. Again, there were considerable regional variations. In Kilrush, County Clare, population losses were estimated to be over fifty per cent of the population. Throughout Ulster, population losses were around seventeen per cent. In counties Fermanagh, Cavan and Monaghan they ranged between twenty-five and thirty per cent. At Inniskeen and Kilsherdany townlands in County Cavan the population fell by thirty-six per cent. Small towns disappeared, and many people left their beloved Ireland. The famine has been described as the result of recession. In 1851 the linen industry had disappeared from many parts of the countryside. In the reasonably prosperous Newtownards Union the famine made a great impact. The weavers in the country were not the same as in pre-famine days. The famine did not end there, for people prayed for good harvests. The people of Ireland – Ulster – did not forget that the policies of the British Government had helped to bring about the famine.

Chapter 1

The Great Hunger in County Antrim

John Lanktree was agent to the Marchioness of Londonderry at the Carnlough and Garron Tower estates from 1842 to 1850. He first mentioned the potato blight in his annual report to Lady Frances Anne in 1845. As with his contemporaries, he was confused by what could be defined as a serious blight and he referred to it as the 'cholera of the potato'. He also mentioned an attempt to describe and explain the disease. The year 1845 was unusually rainy and proved hostile to the potato crop. The potato was native to the sunny lands of South America and needed warm weather for ripening. Conditions in Ireland meant potatoes were prone to blight. Frank Craig was told that it was only on wet ground that any potatoes were harvested, but he believed that the ground was dry until the spuds rotted away.

The poor peasants and tenants of these mountainous regions were a great source of anxiety for the guardians. The famine was attributed to divine providence.

In the late summer of 1845, the first signs of disease came to light in several regions in Ireland. Boards of governors became concerned with the implications of this news. The workhouses were largely dependent upon the potato. Ballycastle was the classic example. A meeting of the board of guardians was aware that the poor were dependent upon the potato. The board of governors of the Ballycastle Union, which met in the courthouse on 3 August 1845, formed themselves into a committee to enable paupers to buy food on the cheapest terms. It was decided that money should be raised by private subscriptions. The guardians were of the opinion that much good might be done by helping local farmers.

The poor would mix potato starch with oatmeal and flour to make bread.

In County Antrim the potato famine was only marginally present. The workhouses reported in July 1845 that the potatoes were of an inferior type, and that it was necessary to serve oatmeal for dinner on Tuesdays and Wednesdays. The urgent nature of the famine took some time to surface. Antrim board of guardians accepted Mr Mullen's tender for supplying the workhouse with potatoes from 1 November 1844 to December 1845 – 'cups' for the month of June and July; 'red downs' for August and 'black seddings' at 1s. 6d. per hundredweight. There is no mention of a breed of potato known as 'doe bachs' or 'doe blacks', which was thought to be immune from the blight. The famine thus was not so severe in County Antrim as in other areas.

The Ballymoney board of guardians became aware of the great hardship being caused by the failure of the potato crop. At a meeting held on 27 August 1845 a letter was sent to one George McCartney of Lisanre Castle suggesting that they undertook the preparation of Indian meal for the poor. There was much discussion, and it was agreed that the workhouse should buy two hundredweight of Indian meal to see if it was suitable for the poor. At another meeting it was reported that the inmates had tried the corn and that they were satisfied with it. It was then agreed that one hundredweight of Indian meal be bought for the next week's consumption. This cost 12s. 6d. per bag.

In early September 1845 the master at Ballymoney was concerned that the potatoes in the fields were vulnerable. A substitute had to be found, and he tried Indian meal in equal quantities with oatmeal to feed the poor. There were appeals from the officers of the workhouse asking what they would be allowed instead of the potato for dinner. It was resolved that they should obtain one shilling's worth of bread in lieu of potatoes.

In October 1845 the master at the Ballymoney workhouse advised the board of guardians that it would not be advisable to buy potatoes at one shilling per bushel and not to use the potatoes in the workhouse grounds when they could be bought at a cheaper price. It was advised that the members should purchase potatoes at a price not higher than one shilling per bushel until further notice. At a meeting held on 8 October 1845, the master reported that on the previous Sunday one third of the spuds could not be used because of the rot. He asked if he was allowed to have additional quantities if he considered it necessary. At the same meeting a tender was received from James Cameron for seven coffins at five shillings and for 'dead dresses' at £1 10s. 4d.

By October 1845 the failure of the potato crop could not be avoided.

There was a full meeting of the Ballymoney guardians on Thursday 12 October. It seemed as if the guardians were unaware of the scarcity of good potatoes and most of the blame was laid at the door of the supplier. He was probably doing his best to fulfil the terms of the contract in adverse circumstances. On 7 October the Poor Law Commissioners authorized all unions in Ireland to depart from the established diets by using oatmeal, rice, bread and other foods in lieu of potatoes wherever the guardians deemed fit. A letter from the Poor Law Commissioners in Dublin was accompanied by an order permitting a change in diet in the workhouses when the potatoes were too bad. Soup was made from vegetables, oatmeal and rice; and pudding was made of any grain. By December the master, Robert Bogle, reported that he had tried a starch made from potatoes in place of meal. He had given 10lb of starch in lieu of 14lb of oatmeal, but these measures were not satisfactory. He had given onions four days in the week, and deducted a small amount of milk in place of them. It was resolved that the master's experience with the starch in place of meal and onions should be approved when the potatoes were totally uneatable. Bogle was delighted to have been given the appointment by the Ballymoney guardians. He wrote a letter to the *Coleraine Chronicle* detailing his method of making starch flour.

There was not much starvation at Antrim. There was a meeting of the Antrim board of guardians which reported that the potatoes sold were of good quality. The use of them for dinner was resumed from the current month. Adult paupers were allowed 4lb of potatoes and children 2lb. Soup was administered three days per week. It was proposed to allocate more potatoes for a fit man for dinner, and this would be a marked increase in diet. However, the guardians were a little premature in deciding that the potato situation was improved.

In the following week, it was decided to supply bread, and at the same meeting a circular letter was received from the Poor Law Commissioners, recommending employment for certain categories of workhouse paupers making potato flour or starch and pulp from diseased potatoes.

For the week beginning 20 November 1845 there was an increase in the quantities of potatoes (6,000lb). This suggested that there was optimism about improving the quality of the crop still to be harvested. At the meeting of the board of guardians in the following week it was reported that potatoes that were substandard had been supplied. It was now decided to take legal action. The suppliers should be contacted by the board's solicitors with instructions to write to the contractors and gain their sureties. Meanwhile the master was authorized to buy the necessary supply until further orders. As a result, the suppliers could well have bankrupted themselves in an effort to fulfil their contracts. With the onset of blight at Lisburn there was a bizarre twist to events. The local landlord, the Marquess of Hertford, paid a visit to his estate and was greatly pleased with its orders and consistency. He said in the visitors' book that it was essential to find a substitute for the Irish potato in England. He ordered a hearty dinner to be provided for the paupers at his expense, consisting of beef, carrots and soup, together with currant buns.

The potato was not the main item on the minutes for November. The receipt of a letter about the famine was reported, and as a result regular diets were introduced. The guardians took the view that the contractors to the union should continue to supply good potatoes to the workhouse. The board did not think it necessary to make a change in diet as yet. The situation changed somewhat, and Mr Clark, the supplier of the potatoes, wrote to the board saying that he had now delivered all the potatoes that he had, for the disease was now widespread. He wanted to be relieved from his contract, which was to expire on 8 March. The board moved quickly and ordered the release of Mr Clark from his contract for potatoes. By late February there was insufficient sustenance in the area. The guardians directed that soup and bread should be provided for dinner four days a week until potatoes could be procured.

Times were difficult for the boards of guardians as they searched for suitable substitutes for potatoes. The Antrim board ordered bread composed of one half Indian meal and one half flour, but it was found to be unfit for use. The contractors said they were unable to meet requirements. It was resolved that the supply of this bread be discontinued and that ordinary bread be substituted.

The Larne guardians seem to have avoided a full-scale failure in the crop of potatoes. The visiting committee, in April 1846, said that the potatoes and milk were of the highest quality. Many complaints were heard by the committee against the Indian meal from paupers, and they recommended that the matter should be reconsidered.

The manifestation of the blight was different in the north and south of the county, as seen in the Ballymoney, Ballycastle, Antrim and Lisburn workhouses; but there was an overall unity in the readiness of the boards of guardians to combat failure of the crop. The people in County Antrim adapted to occasional food shortages. Thirty years prior to 1848 there had been hard times, beginning with the effects of the French wars in Ireland, which had resulted in agricultural depression; County Antrim had therefore escaped the rigours of the Great Hunger and the severe fever that so often accompanied it.

By 1823 a number of the gentry at Ballycastle wanted to set up a dispensary. The first year's subscription amounted to £23 4s. 9d., and other years' were on a similar scale. By 1843 an Act of Parliament empowered the grand jury to make voluntary subscriptions. The Ballycastle Dispensary Committee set up a temporary fever hospital at Bath Lodge on the Shore Road. The building had been a salt store – part of the salt industry that had existed for centuries. It was hoped that the residents of the stone house might escape the fever. The first year's report said that there were twelve patients, two of whom had been cured. The remainder were declared as convalescent.

A number of people were attacked at Ballycastle, where they were resident, and the spread of the disease had been arrested. A stalemate had been reached. In 1839 there were 720 home visits and the number of fever places was 101. The Ballycastle workhouse opened on 18 March 1843. However, the Ballycastle Dispensary Committee continued its good works. By 1 June 1845 the number of cases attended to was given as 714, of whom ten had died.

At Glenarm a fund had been set up for the poor and needy in 1817, during the severe shortages experienced that year. The gentry were generous in their contributions, as they were at Ballycastle. The fund still operated, but by 1841 the situation had changed. It was decided that it would be more beneficial to spend money that had been set aside to purchase food and milk in quantity. This was the beginning of the Glenarm Soup Kitchen. Jeremy Irvine described the situation at Glenarm. He said that the Countess of Antrim subscribed £20, and others subscribed £10 and £20. This enabled the committee to buy stores and equipment. Initial bills included oatmeal at £1 12s. and included a variety of different commodities at lesser prices.

To begin with, the management of the soup kitchen was in the hands of the Court of Vestry. In due course the committee was extended to include the Presbyterian minister, Reverend Alexander Montgomery, and the parish priest, Reverend Michael O'Hagan. By 1847 the famine struck and all the churches at Glenarm were able to work together in the face of starvation. The scheme was highly successful. The Glenarm Soup Kitchen was able to continue without having to seek aid from the government under the terms of the Relief Act. A number of soup kitchens had also been established at Ballintoy, Ballyvennaght, Dunouragan near Caledon, and at the top of Coole Brae in a building which later became a school. Each of these was referred to as 'The Hungry House'. At Ballymena there were soup kitchens at Dundermot, Aghyoghill,

Clough, Broughshane, Kells and Toome. Days were set aside for cooking, and on one day raw meat was provided. The usefulness of the soup kitchens in providing local support was recognized. They provided a lifeline for the poor, including the tenants in North Antrim.

During December 1846, Mr Moore, a member of the Ballycastle board of guardians, attended a meeting of the Coleraine board of guardians to explain the benefits obtained in the Ballycastle Union – ovens had been erected in the workhouses and the soup kitchens throughout the union. The Coleraine guardians spent a lot of their time examining the possibility of providing an oven and a soup kitchen. At another meeting it was reported that a letter received from the Poor Law Commissioners with reference to the minutes of the previous meeting assured people that the soup kitchen would continue to operate in their area.

The Ballycastle board of guardians erected several soup kitchens. An article in the *Coleraine Chronicle* in 1847 said that the workhouse ranked amongst the best in Ireland, and the guardians had set a noble example to other unions. Resolutions were passed in November directing that soup kitchens be established immediately in various parts of the union, where the poor could be looked after.

The Poor Law Commissioners were alarmed at this bold step. They sent an inspector to remonstrate on the consequences. The guardians remained firm until they found that the commissioners were likely to file a suit in Chancery against them. Within a month the situation had become very serious. The government had to change its policy towards the end of January 1847 – and the result was the Temporary Relief Act of Destitute Persons (Ireland) Act. It was known as the Soup Kitchen Act, and it provided for the setting-up of relief committees under the guardians of a new relief commission throughout the country. It would provide food for those unable to gain admission to the workhouse. The relief was to be confined to those attending in person.

The potato crop failed for the second time in 1846. A great flood of starving people made their way into the workhouses, preferring to accept the harsh conditions (including loss of property and the break-up of their family) rather than starve to death in their hovels. In December 1846 the Home Secretary was informed that fifty-six out of 130 workhouses in Ireland were full to capacity, or with far more poor than they were built to accommodate. The government was alarmed, and some means to control the situation was sought. The Ballymoney board of guardians, at a meeting on 31 December 1846, held a discussion in respect of the setting-up of soup kitchens. It was planned that expenses should be supported out of the rates. The gentlemen in the areas where the soup kitchens were established were taxed at a rate of 3d. in the pound in the Poor Law valuation for the purpose of supporting the expenses of the soup kitchens.

In the *Coleraine Chronicle*, in early June 1847, it was said that the board of guardians at Ballycastle had to close the doors of the workhouse, leaving the poor out in the cold. There were 520 inmates in a building that was erected to accommodate 300. Those who had earlier complained about the shortcomings of the workhouses had their answer. In the following week the board of guardians found it necessary to hold a public meeting at Ballycastle Courthouse for the purpose of raising funds for outdoor relief. There was considerable discussion. It was agreed that tenants should pay 6d. in the pound and that landlords should pay one shilling in the pound in the Poor Law valuation of their property. The fact was that (as statistical evidence shows) of the seven workhouses which served Antrim, Ballycastle, Ballymena, Ballymoney, Belfast, Larne and Lisburn only Ballycastle exceeded the limit (300). Here the impact of the famine was most strongly felt in 1847 and 1848. At Larne, Ballymena, Antrim and Ballymoney the numbers were close to the official limit.

Pressure on the workhouses was seasonal until 1847–8. Fever now became rampant as more and more came forward for shelter. The County Antrim workhouses remained under pressure in 1849. This is illustrated in the testimony of Edward Senior, a Poor Law commissioner with responsibility for seventeen unions in the northern area to the select committee on the Poor Law (Ireland) Act in March 1849. He gave the example of the Antrim workhouse to show that workhouse populations were dominated by women, young people and males who could not support themselves.

Of one thousand inmates in a workhouse there were only ten able-bodied people. In 1849 the Antrim workhouse contained 790 inmates, of which there were 125 male adults and 205 female adults – a total of 330 adults. The boys numbered 231, the girls 204, the infants 25. At this time there were only twenty able-bodied men.

The principal way of obtaining food centred on the role of the landlords of County Antrim. They made additional contributions based on the value of their property. The biggest landlords in County Antrim were the Marchioness of Londonderry, Lord Antrim and Lord Hertford. All carried out their duties in regard to their tenants. John Lanktree informed the Marchioness of Londonderry, though she was absent, about her County Antrim estates for a good part of the year. Her attention was drawn to the early manifestations of the blight in 1845. He reported to Lady Frances Anne the following year and lamented that the failure of the 1845 crop of potatoes was starting to be acutely felt. In the Drumcrow area there were a great number of peasants near to starvation. Later, in 1846, he wrote to the Marchioness of Londonderry referring to Sir Robert Peel's policy to import £100,000 worth of Indian meal from America, and he told the Marchioness that they were running out of food. If Peel acted, the situation might be saved.

Lanktree had great difficulty in compiling the annual report for 1847, and he wrote that the Antrim estate for the year 1847 was unfortunately barren of improvements. The famine was said to be the worst in living memory, the suffering terrible. Pallor and anxiety appeared on every side. The Marquess and Marchioness of Londonderry possessed estates throughout Ulster – Down, Donegal, Londonderry and, of course, County Antrim. They lived for most of the year at either of their houses – Wynyard Park in County Durham or Holdernesse House in London. They visited for the first time the Glens of Antrim estate in December 1846, and they said that the people were friendly. Small potatoes were cultivated on this estate. On the mountainsides dependence on the potato was widespread. During their tour, the Londonderrys visited their tenants in the townland of Ballymacaldrack in Dunloy. The tenants were aware of the intended visit and made them welcome with a specially prepared address, written so that it would not offend the visitors. Most of the address praised the thoughtfulness of the landlords in visiting the area. They criticized their former landlords, who had few intentions of remaining loyal to their poor tenants. The Londonderrys said that they would take a great interest in the state of the countryside and towns during the famine. Clothing and blankets were to be provided and cleanliness brought to notice. Rents were to be remitted for the land affected by the Great Hunger. Seed corn was distributed in the spring to the poor of County Antrim. In places the poor tenants had consumed all their grain. Turnip, carrot and parsnip seeds were distributed to all. A large supply of guano was set aside to encourage the cultivation of green crops. An estate committee was established in the Glencloy area. Lady Frances Anne organized a number of charitable functions in England. She and her husband hosted a great military bazaar at Regent's Park Barracks for the distressed. This raised £300. John Lanktree's report in 1848 said that the potato failure had brought chronic problems for some small farmers and ruin was inevitable.

Emigration to America became widespread in the spring of 1848, and there were famine ships in the region of the Scots isles. For example, the *Exmouth* sailed in the same year as Hugh Gullian of Ballymacaldrack succumbed to starvation. Another victim was a woman, and when a post-mortem was carried out on her there was not a morsel in her stomach.

Charles Kelly of Ballyvaddy near Carnlough died. He was the head of a large family that had four cows, two horses and a flock of sheep. He did not want to part with them, and he went through the county begging for himself. He left his family to fend for themselves. He got little encouragement and died on the road.

Lanktree, like others who were interested in modernizing their estates, looked to the benefits that might come from the famine. He spoke about small farms being vacated. Some farms were enlarged, and these were often in the possession of the better sort of farmer-labourer. Of course some had vacated their farms in the face of the Great Hunger.

The Marchioness of Londonderry, despite the famine, went ahead with the building of Garron Tower in 1848. It was a cherished project. This was in the same year that she and Lord Londonderry carried out lavish alterations to Holdernesse House, their London home. In memory of her tenants during the famine, she donated a large, smooth, inscribed block of limestone, which is now known as the Famine Stone. It stands along the Antrim Coast Road, just below Garron Tower. She intended that the stone should be a memorial to Ireland's affliction and England's generosity in the years 1845-7. She described the famine as the worst in Irish history and human suffering.

However, a year later a less favourable side of her personality came to light. John Lanktree had been acting as agent for her, and he had acquired the tenancy of the land in the townland of Stony Hill. Like many other tenants he fell into arrears of rent. As the agent, he tried to serve the interests of his townland, but as a tenant he was bound to support the actions of his fellow tenants. He found himself requesting a lowering of rent on the estate.

Lady Londonderry replied scathingly. She said that Lanktree's principle should be to rent land out as a free gift and ask no rent, as the tenants had not received sixpence. Lanktree replied on 2 July 1850 and pointed out that Lady Londonderry was very charitable and a leading light in the fight against famine in County Antrim. Lanktree found that he had risked everything. The Marchioness acted promptly to have him evicted and sought immediate payment of debts. On 1 February 1851 he was forced to sell his property. He was bankrupt and emigrated with his family to Australia.

Other landlords showed some compassion for their tenants by waiving rent during the worst famine years. One of these was O'Neill of Randalstown, a generous giver. He made grants to local societies. A newspaper report described how Lord Masserene of Antrim sowed some potatoes at the staggering price of £36 per acre. The potatoes looked all right, but a report in the *Belfast Protestant Journal* pointed out that the field was rampant with disease. Lord Masserene gave orders to his steward to release relevant parties, and the agreement could be waived. Lord Masserene was congratulated for his well-timed liberties and humane considerations.

Rathlin Island, off the north coast of Antrim, and separated from the mainland by a three-mile stretch of water, did not escape the famine. In 1851, Mrs Catherine Gage, the wife of the Reverend Robert Gage, a Church of Ireland rector and a landlord of Rathlin, wrote its history. Writing in the closing years of the Great Hunger, she said that the inhabitants were leaving for America. The number of emigrants in the following spring amounted to 107, leaving Rathlin a bit of a wilderness. As on the mainland, the potatoes rotted in the ground.

The Gages were well connected, and appeals for relief met with a good response. A firm of undertakers in Glasgow apologized that they could not assist people who had been shipwrecked. They enclosed a donation of £10 for the islanders to deal with shipwrecks. In April 1847, J. & J. Cooke, who were merchants and shipowners, wrote from Londonderry to the Reverend Robert Gage of Rathlin Island, pointing out that the number of people whom Gage wanted to send to the New World was too much for one ship. The letter referred to Mrs Gage's letters in which she stated that there would be eighty persons or thereabouts emigrating. She said that she would take them all in the ship and that she would do this with pleasure. She said that the number going was great. It was the spring, and Mrs Gage also referred to 107 people emigrating in the spring of 1847. This would appear to confirm that after all J. & J. Cooke was able to accommodate all the islanders fleeing from the famine after the terrible winter of 1846/7. There is a stone at the upper end of Rathlin Island known as the Wintry Stone. On it there is a list of leading figures leaving Rathlin at this time. The passenger lists of J. & J. Cooke reveal that eighty people sailed in the *John Clarke Napier* for Newfoundland on 18 May 1847.

The population of Rathlin Island had begun to decline before the coming of the famine. It dropped from 1,600 in 1841 to 753 by 1851. This was a percentage fall well in excess of the rest of Ireland. Whenever a ship came to the island, the Irish made their way to the docks. It was said that the landlord was not very sympathetic, but this description of the landlord does not tally with that provided by the Reverend H. I. Law, who wrote that the Reverend Robert Gage was faithful to his duties, both to his tenants and to parishioners. During the potato famine of 1847–8 he made great efforts to alleviate the distress of the Gaels of Rathlin. His account of the position was very matter-of-fact. He recorded the various ships that arrived to take the refugees or to bring provisions.

Reverend J. H. Todd, from London, wrote to Gage in 1848 giving some idea of the people's reaction to the famine in Ireland. He said that he could not obtain much finance for the Irish. If the potatoes should fail again that year, he further pointed out that English sympathy would tend to dry up.

The famine in Rathlin is well documented, and it is an important source of information. How they managed food was pointed out: seaweed was boiled with the meagre rations of potatoes that were available. The poor diet caused rashes and probably cholera. No one had whole potatoes.

Those living in coastal areas spent some time gathering seafood to supplement the diet of potatoes. Other items that were not normally used were pressed into service. Limpets were found on the rocks and used in making soup; sloak was boiled and eaten along with dumplings made out of oatmeal. Dulse was also eaten – purple in colour when harvested, it turned green when it was boiled, and made a delicious meal with spuds. In the absence of potatoes it was a poor substitute. Carrageen moss, a seaweed, was generally used as a medicine, but in the famine years it was used as a food. Those who could fish caught lythe, glashan, codlings, mackerel and crabs. There were large numbers of people searching after the same items. It was recorded that on Rathlin Island there were long memories of the famine. Boats would come into the bay and take away over one hundred people, including whole families. Many died on the boat going over.

There are folk memories of the famine in County Antrim itself, and these are very interesting. Descendants of the victims learnt about the privations of the famine period. More than one case was recorded of a person falling into a coma and being taken for dead, but reviving suddenly at the funeral. There were memories of the soup kitchens.

The Great Hunger is usually taken as an event of the 1845–7 period. In Antrim there were signs of the potato blight occurring as late as the 1850s. On 21 December it was resolved by the Lisburn board of guardians that stirabout should be substituted for potatoes on Tuesdays. There was more severe fever at the Antrim Union in September 1851 when there was much suffering and lack of sustenance. By 1852 it was recorded that the blight appeared to be more extensive and severe throughout the union than in other years. These events gave rise to a fear of famine for many years to come.

Chapter 2

The Great Hunger in County Armagh

Robert Dollins observed at a meeting in Lurgan in 1849 that those suffering from the famine had brought it upon themselves by laziness and indolence. He claimed that the famine did not affect occupied people in the north due to their ability to sustain themselves in such situations. Two years earlier, the population of North Armagh had suffered severely along with their brethren in the south and west, with little assistance forthcoming from gentlemen such as Mr Dollins. By the 1840s County Armagh was the most densely populated county in Ireland. It had experienced the great troubles which faced the rural communities following the Napoleonic wars. Prior to the famine technical innovations had severely undermined the economic well-being of weavers and their families. In the years 1846–8 there was a slump in the trade, especially in the demand for cotton. A Belfast newspaper reported that mill construction was abandoned in the city. Those partially built were left unfinished. The situation was serious, and in May 1847 the *Northern Whig* proclaimed that productive industry was paralysed, and the working man and the working woman were left dependent on charity.

During March the *Northern Whig* reported that the flax crop had proven to be much smaller than usual, with the result that flax was so dear and scarce that it could not be obtained even if the spinners could afford the high prices. The oat crop used by the wealthy families as an alternative to potatoes proved to be more useful than was first thought. By March 1847 the price of oats had more than doubled to 20s. 6d. per hundredweight. A chance combination of a slump in demand, together with poor flax and oat harvests, only exaggerated the problems already being experienced by weaving communities.

At Lurgan the Poor Law was constituted under the Poor Law Act of 1838. This covered much of North Armagh as well as parts of counties Antrim and Down. It contained in 1841 a population of around 71,128, living in an area of 79,201 acres. There were many weavers' cottages to small plots of land. Landholdings of one acre or less made up over one third of the total number of landholdings in the union. This was related to the state of the linen industry in the area. John Hancock, agent to Charles Brownlow, the local landlord, presented his opinions to the Devon Commission in 1844. Linen manufacture offered the strongest inducement to subdivision. A small plot of land, in addition to looms, would support a family.

Alongside the weavers there resided a substantial number of people who lived on the margin of existence. Over one third of the population managed to eke out a living as basic as anywhere else in Ireland. This means of employment was only to be had during the harvest period. Wages averaged about one shilling per day. When out of work they went begging and relied upon charity. They lived in one-roomed mud cabins with little furniture, whilst their clothing was wretched beyond description. Their diet consisted almost entirely of potatoes and milk. There were additions of salted herrings, oatbread and stirabout. The use of meal was virtually unheard of. The Reverend Iver of Tartaraghan stated that sometimes their breakfast, dinner and supper consisted of potatoes. Although Lurgan had a great reputation for linen manufacture, there were a substantial number of people living at the lowest level.

The Lurgan workhouse opened on 22 February 1841 and was filled with 800 poor. But from then until 1845 the house was not one quarter filled. A husband and wife adopted the roles of the master and matron, and a sound administrative system was carried out in these years. In May 1843 the husband and wife were dismissed for suspected 'levity of conduct'! This was a highly significant event, for the following years witnessed the appointment of three different masters, who did little to bring about a smooth-running administration. In the midst of this change the workhouse received its first test with the outbreak of famine in June 1846. The workhouse was substantially filled with about 500 poor, many of whom were from the fever hospital. Dr Stevens of the Fever Commission paid a visit to Dublin, and in his report he gave details of how the medical officer, Dr Bell, had been permitting the children of the sick to enter the hospital. This exacerbated an already deteriorating situation.

The Fever Commission wrote to the Lurgan board of guardians to demand the resignation of Bell. The guardians were not well pleased with what they saw as interference in their internal affairs. They presented a vigorous defence. The defence was so vigorous, in fact, that the commissioners left the final decision to the guardians themselves. Dr Bell's salary was increased by £20 per annum, but, unknown to the guardians, the negligence of their medical officer was to have far-reaching consequences in the months that lay ahead. Many people were now applying for admission to the workhouse.

The first failure of the potato crop was in 1845, but it was not as serious as in other regions. This had an impact on the Lurgan Union. James Woodhouse, a local businessman, reported substantial losses in crops in the Portadown area. There was a supply of potatoes in the Lurgan workhouse, but these were insufficient, for a large number of them were rotting, and many were small. One of the leading consequences of the potato blight was that there was an increase in the price of the potatoes per hundredweight, from 1s. 11d. in April 1845 to 2s. 3d. in March 1846. The amount of potato declined in the workhouse diet, being replaced at first by bread rather than meal. In April 1846 dinner consisted of a few ounces of meal made into stirabout.

Another failure of the crop occurred in 1845, and this resulted in a shortfall of some ten per cent in the supply of seed potatoes for the following year.

In 1846 the new crop appeared to be blight-free. A local constabulary report stated that many persons had decided on not planting potatoes to a great extent, but that they had changed their minds when they found that those planted were healthy and vigorous in growth. In April the grand jurors of County Armagh reported favourably about the crop.

Their optimism was unfounded, since in July and August the potato blight struck again, this time with widespread and devastating effect. The *Northern Whig*, quoting from an agricultural report, stated that, as far as the eye could see in the Armagh fields, there was disease everywhere. The flowers of the potato withered. This report was confirmed by a Mr Brown from Donacloney, who informed the Lurgan Union Farming Society that from Warrenpoint to Lurgan he could smell rotten potatoes. The Lurgan Union did not escape the blight, so the commissioners recalled. The blight reappeared in every electoral division and affected whole crops.

There was an increase in the number entering the workhouse. At the end of September 1846 the number was 313; by October it reached 432; by November 598; and by the close of December the workhouse was full, with 805 inmates. A number of inmates died and their places were taken by more of the poor. The average number of deaths per month throughout the year was about fourteen, but in November 1846 thirty-one paupers died, and in December fifty-eight deaths occurred.

The Poor Law was perhaps overwhelmed by the large numbers wanting relief. The workhouses were not built to withstand a famine such as that of the mid-nineteenth century. They did not realize the full extent of the calamity. It was, however, thought that the potato famine had made small farmers lazy. A number of landlords believed this and did not take pity on the plight of the poor. From March 1846 to March 1847 only eleven of the thirty-two guardians attended more than half of the fifty-four meetings. Some attended forty meetings or more. There was apathy and a disinterest about those dying in the workhouse between December 1846 and April 1847. The guardians were ignorant of the conditions in the workhouse. They paid little attention to the quality of the food served to the paupers and administration was strict; but it was of the utmost importance that they should not be negligent. Father O'Brien discovered a corpse that had been dead for sixteen hours. He declared that this was an outrageous state of affairs and a 'dereliction of duty'. It was a symptom of earlier problems.

The Lurgan Union was not by itself in its suffering. On 6 January 1847 a Belfast newspaper reported that Ireland was suffering from a great calamity – famine, disease and death were prevailing almost everywhere. There were accounts of destitution and death in their most extreme form. The cries of suffering people were becoming more pronounced each day and the prospects for the future were dark. The workhouse was full and the cries of distress were answered by the setting-up of local relief committees. These committees responded to the conditions in many part of Ireland after the crop failure of 1845, but they proved to be unnecessary in most of Ulster. Conditions worsened in the winter of 1846, and the relief committees proved to be vital in the effort to bring food to the poor. The Poor Law was restricted to conditions within the workhouses, and it was totally hopeless with regard to distress elsewhere.

By December relief organizations had been set up at Lurgan, Portadown, Drumcree, Clonmakate and Moira. In January further groups were set up at Donacloney, Tullylish, Maralin, Ballinderry and Kernan. At Drumcree the condition of the poor was described as desperate, and also at Portadown. Lord Gosford declared that the population was very dense and in a most wretched condition. Conditions at Donacloney were also desperate. At Moira the destitute condition of the poor was commented upon. Those responsible for the setting-up of relief were both Protestant and Catholic. The landlords cooperated at a minor level or solely through subscription. The relief committees' task was to distribute food – mainly meal and soup – and any amount subscribed was augmented by central government funds in Dublin. Clergymen, gentry and farmers made up the number of subscribers, and they played a leading role in ameliorating the effects of the famine at local level. The following agencies supported the Lurgan Union: the Belfast Relief Fund; the Central Relief Committee of the Society of Friends; the National Fund (London); the Ladies' Dublin Association; the Durham Relief Association; the Irish Relief Association and the Calcutta Fund.

It was said that some of the landlords did not care about the condition of their tenants. In a letter to a local paper, the Reverend Clements of Tartaraghan complained profusely about the callousness of local landlords. He said that there were only two landed proprietors living within the parish. A large estate went bankrupt as a result of debt. A large part of the parish was bog belonging to absentee landlords, and upon the bog lived a large number of the most wretched tenants, who had not been assisted by the landlords.

There was red tape, which meant that there was delay in bringing about relief. A possible explanation was that the Relief Commissioners at Dublin were busy with requests for aid. The local committees sent letters to the authorities, telling them of the amount subscribed locally, and inquiring when the government would send more money. On 28 March William Morris, local potentate and treasurer of the Lurgan Relief Fund, send a letter to Dublin stating that £53 had been contributed and asking for a similar amount. At Ballinderry, the treasurer wrote to Dublin, but by the beginning of March he had heard nothing.

The local relief committees, despite the obstacles, carried out their duties well in distributing food. The Anglican rector in Lurgan, the Reverend Oulton, sold good nourishing broth at one penny per quart. The Drumcree Fund distributed food weekly to about 450 poor families, amounting to 2,300 people. Babington, the secretary, commented that there was not a single family left without assistance. Without it many would have died. In Ballinderry, Indian meal, which had been outlawed by the Treasury, provided relief at half price. In Donacloney, Kernan and Moira, soup was being distributed throughout local kitchens with the Kernan committee supplying about 300 people. One of the most affected areas was Tartaraghan where the Reverend Clements condemned the evils of absenteeism. A soup kitchen had been established to serve 1,300 persons – a figure that was expected to increase daily.

Clements sent word to Dublin about the state of hunger in the locality. Starvation was widespread on the farms, and many were living on one meal a day, made up of herbs and vegetables. Vagabonds wandered the countryside demanding assistance. In the absence of public works of any kind, it was hard to know where to begin. Some resorted to obtaining food illegally. In January 1846 the police in Portadown reported that a number of men had stolen fifty bags of flour from a barge at Madden's Bridge. In the following week other thefts took place from boats of the Dublin Canal Company, in which barrels of flour and Indian meal were stored. There was a subsequent meeting of the county magistrates, and outrage was expressed at the thefts. Gentlemen, however, believed that the police were totally inadequate in strength to take the 'duty-keeping watch'. It was essential to stop these activities by the Irish, so a portion of His Majesty's troops were usefully employed in protecting the boats filled with provisions on the Newry Canal.

The vast majority of Irish stood within the confines of the law; and, for many, the only aid available was from the local workhouses. Here daily deaths were commonplace. In the first week of January there were eighteen deaths; in the second week the number was thirty-six, and for the week ending 16 January the total was fifty-five deaths. The visiting chaplain's notebooks recorded a sorry tale of burials, with both Anglican, Presbyterian and Catholic priests performing burials daily. The Dublin Commissioners expressed concern, and on 16 January they sent a letter to the Lurgan guardians expressing their regret at what had passed at the workhouse. They demanded a detailed report from Dr Bell explaining why there was so much mortality. In May 1846 Dr Stevens asked for a report on the sanitary conditions in the workhouse. Bell claimed that the number of deaths had been caused by the large numbers of refugees who had died shortly after admittance. It was a well-known fact that many of the dying were sent for admission merely that coffins could be obtained for them at the expense of the union.

In regard to sanitation, Bell reported that there were four times the normal number of inmates, and the building was overcrowded. It was impossible to provide dry bedding, so sleeping on damp beds was common, and this would have worsened the fever. Bowel cases sometimes proved fatal. The doctor reached the conclusion that this cause of death could be largely eradicated by the buying of new bedding and the making of a proper drying house. It is not clear whether this statement was meant to placate the commissioners or not.

It was soon seen to be impracticable to avoid the high mortality levels, which continued to increase. In the week ending 23 January 1847, fifty-eight perished and the bread was bad. On 30 January there were sixty-eight deaths; on 6 February ninety-five; and on 13 February sixty-seven. The large number of deaths at the Lurgan workhouse was the highest in

Ulster, representing about one fifth of the total mortality for that week (529 dead). The second highest figure was thirty deaths in the Enniskillen workhouse. The largest number of all was in the south of Ireland in the Cork Union, where the workhouse population stood at 5,388, and where 128 deaths had occurred. In Connaught the highest death rate was at the Loughrea workhouse in County Galway; out of 524 inmates, twenty-six had perished.

Sixty-seven deaths occurred in Lurgan in the following week and this was closely behind the figure for County Donegal. Here there were 426 inmates, and sixty-nine died. The largest figure was again in Cork, where 164 perished.

Glenties was declared to be one of the most distressed areas by the British Relief Association. Large-scale relief was required to keep the wolf from the door. At the same time Cork became synonymous with the ravages of the famine. There were mass famine graves. In the early months of 1847 the Lurgan area was suffering great losses on a par with the most affected areas of the rest of Ireland. Normally it was a prosperous and thriving town.

Dr Bell declared that many deaths had occurred as the result of wet beds, but this does not appear to be a satisfactory explanation, for members of the staff had started to become sick. By late January dysentery was rife. Staff and inmates all fell under the fever. In February the assistant master died, and the clerk was suffering from severe symptoms of dysentery. The guardians said that the situation was desperate and two remedies were attempted. The first remedy was that all available space was to be utilized in order to avoid overcrowding. The aged, and infirm women were moved to a room above the stairs, and the women's day room was required for hospital paupers. The guardians thought that more drastic measures should be taken. On 5 February they issued an announcement that the doors of their workhouse and fever hospital would be closed against any further admissions.

Three well-known physicians were called in to remedy the extent and seriousness of the disease. Doctors Thompson, Cumming and Purdon recommended that another doctor, along with Dr Bell and Dr McVeagh, was essential to deal with the situation. They said that the present pauper diet was inadequate: soup only was served up for dinner and four ounces of rice with bread and buttermilk for supper.

The doctors recommended a strict food ration: breakfast, three and a half ounces of meal and porridge, and one quarter-pint of buttermilk; dinner, six ounces of bread and one pint of broth; supper, three ounces

33

of bread and one quarter-pint of buttermilk. They also demanded that the porridge be made entirely of oatmeal, not Indian meal.

The authorities had great problems in dealing with the plight of the poor, and they were concerned about the closure of the workhouse to more sick. In a communication to the Relief Commission's office in Dublin, John Hancock reported that, out of 313 cases on the books of the Lurgan Dispensary, 136 were sick with fever and dysentery. For the same period in 1846 the total was twenty. The extent of the epidemic may be measured by Hancock's enquiry as to whether the Central Board of Health should appoint a medical officer to provide food and medicines for the poor and destitute living in their own homes.

No reply to this letter has survived, but it illustrates the alarming extent to which fever and disease had become widespread in the Lurgan area. Concerned people like Hancock felt themselves helpless. The belief that the disease remained rampant, and would not be blamed upon the authorities, was challenged by two devastating and condemning investigations. One case was from within the workhouse, the other from without. They cast great doubt over the competence of the doctors and the administrative staff in the workhouse.

The deaths soon reached the attention of the press. Under the headline 'Mortality in the Lurgan workhouse', the *Newry Telegraph* reported on the mortality rate and the fact that many office holders, as well as the sick, had been, or were, ill. The *Belfast Vindicator* informed its readers that nearly 400 poor had died in the Lurgan workhouse during the previous eight weeks. The commissioners had been watching the situation, and were obviously not in agreement with Dr Bell's report. They decided to send Dr Smith from the Central Board of Health to look into conditions in the workhouse. Smith had only visited two other workhouses – Bantry and Cork. He now made a 300-mile journey north to observe conditions at Armagh. The commissioners were determined to bring about relief immediately. Dr Smith completed his report on 17 February and commented upon the extent of medical care in the workhouse: overcrowding was a great problem and this was blamed on the general administration in the buildings. Smith reported that in male and female infirmaries there was an average of two persons to each bed, and three or four to a bed was not uncommon. The wards were in a shocking condition. The beds lay upon wet ground and people were dying in them. The clothes were filthy and the ventilation inadequate.

Other investigations found the floor and walls of the infirmary to be in a very poor state. The windows were closed, the atmosphere foul. Walls had not been whitewashed and buckets were used as lavatories.

They were left for hours without being emptied. Drinks were served, presumably at regular intervals.

A similar scene was met by the doctor in the fever sheds. But the fever hospital, controlled by a full-time nurse, was found to have comfortable beds, and clean walls and floors. The wards were well ventilated and the patients were well attended to.

As a result of the chronic overcrowding at Armagh, there was an inadequate supply of garments, and there were only the clothes of the poor who had died of the fever or dysentery. Burials proved a problem. Many of the poor had been buried less than four yards from the fever hospital. In the centre of the graveyard was the well which supplied water to the workhouse. The graves had been dug so close to it that the water had become foul. Smith described the Lurgan workhouse as a disgrace, and said that he had never witnessed such sickness. He recommended that a number of measures should be forthcoming. No more people were to be admitted to the workhouse, since it was overcrowded, and the rooms used by the sick were to be properly fumigated and whitewashed, along with the cleansing of its floors and improvement in its ventilation. There was to be a daily inspection by the medical officer to see that these measures were carried out.

Smith felt it necessary to apportion blame for the conditions and he recorded that it was very difficult to determine the causes of death in the Lurgan workhouse. He thought that the problem stemmed from the dearth of clean water.

John Meason in early November was dismissed, and three weeks passed before a successor could be found. Overcrowding during this period was a major difficulty and this problem wasn't fully resolved until the end of January. Many subordinate officers became ill themselves and this was said to have been caused by poor ventilation, and lack of cleanliness at a time when the strictest attention to these important matters was in the process of arresting the spread of the fever elsewhere. He concluded that despite efforts to improve conditions in the workhouse, the staff were not overenthusiastic. The activities of Dr Bell had to be considered. The guardians were strict in their surveillance and they tried to prevent more deaths. Dr Smith, however, stated that the guardians had no knowledge of the state of the infirmary in regard to cleanliness and ventilation, etc., either from first-hand experience or otherwise. The reports of the doctors informed them of the overcrowding, which was the only particular about which they were acquainted. Dr Smith made a thorough indictment of the Lurgan workhouse and its administration. He said that he thought that the chief causes of neglect were internal and a result of the ineffective management of the institution.

It was a wide-ranging report, and it served to undermine the position of those charged with the care of the poor in the Lurgan workhouse. Almost immediately afterwards, a letter from the chaplain indicated incompetence and indifference on behalf of both the staff and members of the Lurgan board of guardians. A lengthy letter was sent to Lord Lurgan by the Reverend Oulton, drawing attention to the appalling food served up in the workhouse. He said that it was hardly to be wondered that there should be so much disease in the workhouse if the quality of the food left so much to be desired. He said that the bread used for supper was off, insufficiently baked and sour. The soup was bad and many of the paupers could not eat it. He said that the meat was terrible – something that could be obtained on the Lurgan streets – and that it was only fit for animals. He doubted that the kitchen and utensils were in an acceptable condition. He said that adverse conditions might continue in the workhouse. Oulton concluded his letter by stating that he could not refrain from making these comments in view of the terrible mortality that had set in. It was requested that an investigation should be set up right away.

Almost immediately an investigation was set up by the board, involving many workhouse officials. The ward master, Thomas Lutton, said that the bread had been bad for over a week and that it was not fit for human consumption. Many of the sick paupers complained to him that the bread was so bad that it could not be eaten. He believed their complaints. He said that the beef used for making soup was very poor in quality and reported this to Mr Bullock. He reported that the food smelled bad and that the soup was later sent to patients in the hospital.

There was a stark difference between the lives of the poor and those of the officials, and this is illustrated in Lutton's account: he complained that the burials furnished by the officers were much better than those provided for the poor. This was corroborated by another ward master, William Fairly, who said that the baker, when be brought bread, always had the officials' bread in a basket by itself.

Fairly believed that the paupers' bread was unfit for human consumption, and this was also the view of Dr Bell, who said that the bread was of poor quality for about two months. He also said that the meat had been bad for a long time, though it was not bad at present. He concluded by saying the fever in the workhouse would not have been so bad if there was good bread and good beef. Dr McVeagh believed that diarrhoea and dysentery, now rampant because of the fever, had been exacerbated by substandard bread. In his experience as a medical man, he had never seen worse food than in the Lurgan workhouse, but decent soup was now being served up to the poor.

The consequence of the inquiry was the return of 200lb of bread to the contractor, Kennedy. John Hancock, in his letter to the commissioners, said that only 6lb of meat had been deemed uneatable. An explanation was given for the obvious chaos in the workhouse: the fact that the master and matron had succumbed to the famine. Their duties were being carried out by the schoolmaster and schoolmistress, who were doing as well as could be expected under such circumstances.

The workhouse appears to have had a notorious reputation in the union. This was reflected in a visitation made by Henry Wynne, chairman of the Moira Relief Committee. The mortality in the Lurgan workhouse was such that the guardians were unable to send any poor to the building at that time.

The revelations of these inquiries did not come as a surprise. In February 1846 a visiting committee from the Poor Law Commissioners had described the workhouse as being filthy. Dr Stevens, a few months later, discovered conditions which he believed necessitated the prompt removal of the medical officer. The board of guardians, along with the medical staff, seem to have shown a disregard for the paupers under their care. No steps were taken about cleanliness and the provision of ample medical facilities. The clothes of the diseased who had died had been passed on unwashed to the poor. No attempt was made to ensure a decent standard of living for the paupers. The use of unclean clothes, together with supplies of bad bread and meat, meant that instead of containing the fever and other diseases the famine devastated the workhouse. The incompetence of the administration meant also that the fever could more easily sweep through the building.

Dr Smith pointed out that the lapse between the death of Mr Meason and the appointment of a new master happened at a time when the workhouse numbers were rising rapidly. Between May 1845 and May 1847 there were several masters in the workhouse, but a smooth-running institution was not achieved. Other administrators were also incompetent. They seem to have had no idea of what conditions were like in the workhouse. It took the reports of visiting doctors, together with the reports of other observers, to bring the reality of the situation to notice. No one was prepared to shoulder the blame for the incompetence. Only one member of the staff resigned – Dr Bell. He reported that overwork had caused a deterioration of his own health. It was unlikely that Bell would have been able to continue as medical officer following the reports of his incompetence. His resignation was accepted. By now those responsible for appointing both medical and administrative staff and contractors for food did not feel it necessary to take similar action. No member of the Lurgan board of guardians resigned.

Death and destitution did not only obtain in the workhouse. A local newspaper reported that from the Lurgan workhouse sickness was spreading rapidly outside of its walls. Unless the government stepped in and sent doctors from Dublin to investigate the cases of distemper (and take measures to prevent it) there would be havoc. This prediction proved to be correct. Shortly afterwards the famine claimed its most important casualty – the landlord, Lord Lurgan. He died of typhus fever in April. This sudden setback was lamented in the *Newry Telegraph*, which reported that he was a good landlord and esteemed in Ulster. Care and consideration of his tenants was his main concern. The *Armagh Guardian* said that he united all manner of people, lending an attentive ear to their distress and welfare. However, the *Belfast Vindicator*, although it regretted the late lord's death, painted a more sombre picture. It stated that it was high time that the mighty made common cause with the poor.

Lord Lurgan was given a stately burial. Local dignitaries attended the funeral as well as the rich and the poor. His body was buried in the Brownlow family vault in Shankhill parish graveyard.

Those that perished as a result of the famine received no extravagant treatment. Many of them died by the roadside and in ditches. Lord Lurgan's death received more attention in the press than any of the filthy conditions in the workhouse. The book of deaths recorded the deaths of the paupers in great numbers, but they did not obtain a single burial service. Sometimes coffins were brought to the graveyard carrying two or three dead. Sometimes there were up to twenty bodies in one grave.

This practice did not only apply to the coffins in the workhouse. A member of the Society of Friends, commenting about the conditions in Tartaraghan, in the west of the union, said that the previous year many had been buried without a hearse, and this would have been a lasting stigma to any family. Hearses were now almost completely set aside. Death and disease were rampant in the Lurgan Union. The union was not popular with the local press. The press, appealing to the middle and upper working classes, was more interested in the situation in America, Europe and Africa than in the position of the Lurgan Union and its environs. Without the reports of the various religious societies and the occasional letter to the press, it was easy to be misled into thinking that there was little distress in this area, and that famine conditions were limited to the provinces of Munster and Connaught. Correspondence was limited, and it does not offer a valuable insight into the conditions at Lurgan during the years of trouble.

In a letter, the *Belfast News Letter* records the suffering of the poor. It said that the Christian Friends in England had met with deplorable conditions which exceeded that of the south of Ireland. At about the beginning of April, on the old road leading to Portadown, a reporter called upon a family named McClean, who lived in a house likened to a pigsty. The poor man was put to bed and given assistance, but he died a few days later. His wife met the same fate, their daughter also. The correspondent had reported his visit on a Thursday: he saw a young man about twenty years of age sitting before a coal fire, entirely naked. The family lay on wretched beds, also naked, with old rugs for covering. The eating place was dark. He saw a young man without clothes, his eyes sunk, his mouth wide open, his flesh shrivelled up, the bones all visible, and with a very small waist. The corpse had been left in that condition for five successive days. The same writer visited the house in the following week and ran up against further horrors.

Heart-rending sights were common. In Tartaraghan, the Society of Friends reported that people had perished as a result of starvation. One member commented that a four-year-old girl, who a few weeks before had been in a healthy state, was now so emaciated that she could not stand up. The writer in the paper concluded that she was rapidly approaching death, and that everywhere could be seen the appalling conditions of the needy. He expected to see conditions like those obtaining in County Cork in the south of the country.

The board of guardians, under the watchful eye of the commissioners, began to put their house in order. A new medical officer was appointed, Dr McLoughlin, from Downpatrick. The guardians now decided to improve all aspects of the administration. From now on, the medical officer had to attend each board meeting. He was to report any sickness, mortality, medical requirement or deterioration. The master had to have his books written up and given to the clerk each Tuesday morning for posting to the commissioners that evening. He was required to attend each board meeting with all the necessary books of the workhouse under his control for the information of the board.

As a result of Dr Smith's comments, sanitary improvements were made. The porter was told to burn the clothes of dead paupers, and to cleanse with brimstone and sulphur the clothes of those still living. All ventilators had to be cleansed and improved. On 24 March, Dr Phillips was told that his services were no longer required. On Dr McLoughlin's order the board refused admission to any further paupers until further notice. At the end of March the assistant Poor Law Commissioner, Mr Senior, saw men and women helping themselves to food in the workhouse, not under supervision. The master was accused of being negligent and he replied that he did not believe he was ineffective. The master, Mr Easton, tendered his resignation. Charles Hurde took over but resigned within a week. David Gillespie, who had been the assistant medical officer, was appointed on a temporary basis, but was made permanent master a short time later.

With the appointment of the new master and medical officer, together with initial improvements, the workhouse began to operate more efficiently. This was reflected by a significant reduction in the number of the dying. In early April the medical officer reported typhus as being on the increase.

On 1 May, the weekly board meeting took place at the local courthouse. The Lurgan guardians preferred the building to that of the workhouse, where there was severe fever. The fever appeared to be endemic, both inside and outside the workhouse. Following a letter from Dr Hannay of the Lurgan Dispensary, informing them of the situation in Lurgan and Brownlowderry, the Central Board of Health sent tents to those districts which were badly affected by the fever.

Permission was granted on 22 May and 7 June for the erection of temporary fever hospitals at Moira, Lurgan, Kernan and Portadown, which had beds for 225 patients. The accommodation proved to be insufficient. By 17 June, the medical officer reported widespread sickness, fever, dysentery and bad housing among the poor. As a matter of urgency, further accommodation in the form of sheds and tents was provided; and famine hospitals were established at Portadown Road, Lurgan and at Portadown itself, which housed twenty patients.

Accommodation was further improved by the renting of Greer's distillery at Lurgan, which provided places for 400 poor. It was virtually an ancillary workhouse. Although there were stores in the winter of 1847/8, the authorities were now in a better position to cope with the paupers. By March 1848 over 1,500 poor were being cared for. This increase in the workhouse capacity meant that the fatal overcrowding of the previous year was avoided. Tents were put up and fresh bedding was available. Numbers requiring relief were not high during 1848, and the following year witnessed a great reduction in the workhouse poor and a gradual return to the pre-famine conditions of the early 1840s. Potatoes were reintroduced into the workhouse diet for the first time since 1845. The Great Hunger at Lurgan was over. But why did the poor of the town suffer so badly?

The Lurgan area was thought to be an industrial heartland, so the poor to some extent had industry to fall back upon as the famine receded; but there were still problems arising from the failure of the potato crop. It is important to note that the industrial sector was itself undergoing a period of transformation. Prior to the famine the linen industry, the most important sector of the Lurgan economy, was also undergoing change. Mechanized spinning was going ahead, bringing about the demise of the cottage industries. Many of the weavers had become unemployed. Weavers had become more reliable as supplies of yarn for large-scale manufacture increased, but their ability to negotiate prices had been restricted. The years 1847-8 saw a serious decline in the linen trade. The *Northern Whig* reported that mills were only working to half capacity, with many of the working population thrown out of work and left to seek charity. The construction of new mills was started at Belfast. Those that had just been built were fitted with machinery.

The year 1847 also saw the flax crop attacked by a vegetable bug, resulting in smaller crops and a rise in prices. The spinners, already poor, could not purchase any supplies. It has often been asserted that the weavers' families, having a decent income, were able to enjoy a better diet than that of other labourers. One of the main constituents was oats, but the harvest was less than fifty per cent of that of an average year, so prices rocketed, in some cases to twenty-two shillings per hundredweight – more than twice the normal price.

The role played by the workhouse was of great importance; but it had not been built for a tragedy as severe as the famine. The incompetence of the Lurgan guardians and the officers they appointed only served to exacerbate the problem for those for whom they were responsible. Dr Smith observed that there was no knowledge of the conditions in the workhouse and that the authorities showed little interest in vital concerns, such as the quality of food which had been purchased. Strict administration was of vital importance and standards had to be kept high. The Lurgan workhouse resembled a morgue on either side of Christmas 1846. Improvements to the building were under way, but these only served to accentuate the extent to which inefficient management had contributed to the high mortality rate which had developed out of the ravages of the famine. Long-term structural change had undermined the earnings of the weavers, leaving them at risk. As economic downturn was widespread, the poor were left relying on the oat and flax harvests.

The board of guardians and workhouse officials seemed not to care about the poor. They showed themselves to be incompetent in dealing with sickness. These factors, plus the potato blight in successive years, increased North Armagh's suffering under the ravages of the famine.

Chapter 3

The Great Hunger in County Cavan

During the first half of the nineteenth century, County Cavan had, in common with the rest of Ireland, a population explosion. In 1841 Cavan had a population of 243,158 – an increase of 24.7% in twenty years. The greatest population was in the baronies of South-East Cavan; the lowest was in the mountainous west. Most of the people were very poor and were easy victims of the famine. They depended upon their labour for a living and they were dependent upon the potato. Local food shortages and outbreaks of fever were not unusual in Cavan in the twenty years before the famine. In the 1820s and 1830s there were reports of famine in the land. Recovery was generally immediate but short-lived. Eighty-two percent of the houses in County Cavan had mud walls, thatched, with only one room. There was an absence of furniture, except for perhaps a few stools, a table, a few pots to drink from and a pot for boiling potatoes.

Pierce Morton of Kilnacrott House, a relief worker, described the housing conditions in the parish of Crosserlough before the famine. He said that there were cabins of stone, which were poorly thatched. The floor was made out of clay. In winter, conditions were wet and harsh. Rain fell through the roofs, and the occupants slept in their clothes on dried rushes. The chimney corner was the warmest place in the hovel.

Agriculture in County Cavan had not declined in the aftermath of the Napoleonic Wars. The supply of linen exceeded demand, so wages were depressed – ten pence per day in summer and eight pence per day in winter, amongst the lowest orders in Ulster. Linen as a cottage industry was collapsing in the face of the spinning factories, mainly in the Lagan Valley. This was a process that took place from 1825 onwards. Large numbers of labourers and their families relied on spinning and weaving during the winter to subsidize their incomes, particularly in the centre and south-east of County Cavan, where the flax and linen district centred around Cootehill and Bailieborough. Many of the labourers and small farmers found themselves closer to impoverishment. They were also in the dodgy position of being totally dependent upon the potato. When the potato crop failed in 1845 it had a terrible effect upon the lower classes.

The blight covered most of Cavan in the summer of 1845, but it was not until the crop was harvested in October that the full effect of the blight was realized. Abraham Brush reported that in the vicinity of Cavan town the blight prevailed to an alarming extent. A correspondent in the *Freeman's Journal* reported on 10 November that in many places one third and generally one quarter of the poor man's crop was ruined. From Blacklion in the extreme west of County Cavan, it was also reported on 11 October that the failure was not general, but some pointed to a failure rate of one quarter to one sixth of the crop. From Belturbet in early December the rector in Derryheen reported that one half of the crop had been lost and that there was little chance of the remainder of the crop faring any better. On 6 December the *Freeman's Journal* reported on the plight of Dickson's distillery at Belturbet.

The partial failure of the potato crop in 1845 meant that by the late spring and summer of 1846 large numbers of people had no food. Food had to be provided for the poorest labourers by public works. In this way starvation and death were avoided. As early as February 1846 public meetings were being held in Bailieborough and Ballyjamesduff and many relief committees started to function. Relief committees were also established at Shercock and Killinkere in April, and Cavan town in May. The aim was to collect money for the poor and to select public works to be carried out with the aid of government subsidies. Their membership was made up of local landlords who were resident in County Cavan.

Catastrophe now loomed. A county infirmary in Cavan town and three workhouses at Cavan, Cootehill and Bailieborough (opened in 1842) were expected to cope with the deluge of paupers. The seriousness of the situation did not become apparent until early 1846. Cavan workhouse was the biggest of the three, and had room for 1,200 paupers; Bailieborough for 600; and Cootehill for 800. Another five unions had land within County Cavan, but they were soon overcrowded, and fever broke out in them. They were hampered in their efforts to cope with the crisis. Funds were needed and the guardians found it hard to collect the Poor Law rate.

Reports came in of distress from different areas of County Cavan in 1846. James McKieran from Gowna wrote to Sir Robert Peel on 31 January, saying that the potato situation was worse than in any other part of Europe. The supply was not expected to last beyond 1 April. Cattle had died from eating bad potatoes. Street paupers were everywhere and were often in the last stages of their misery. People were starving and immediate relief was necessary. Delay could mean the 'murder of thousands'. Reports in April and May said that one family near Ballyjamesduff was without food or means to gain shelter for two days. The farmers of Crossdoney, who were normally in comfort, were now without food. Near the south of Cavan many farmers were reduced to one meal a day. Pierce Morton spoke of great misery in the Ballyjamesduff area. The condition of the poor was like a nightmare. Patrick O'Reilly in County Cavan, said that in an area of fifty townlands around Cavan there were 250 families (1,131 persons) unemployed and in a state near starvation. In the environs of Cavan there were another 229 families (560 persons) all seeking bread. Mr Tatlow, agent to Mr Nesbitt, provided meals for his tenantry at Crossdoney.

Sessions were held in April 1846 in each of the eight baronies in County Cavan. New parochial relief committees to regulate those already in existence were formed, and a scheme to the value of £11,000, later to be increased to £25,000, was put forward to the Board of Works for approval. A subscription fund was begun, to set against the government loan for these works. The relief works aimed at three areas – roadworks (which began in May and June), drainage and railway construction.

The most extensive drainage project was the cutting of the Ballinamore and Ballyconnell Canal, now known as the Shannon–Erne Link. By September it employed 3,500 at 1s. 8d. per day per labourer. The Erne was drained.

It was suggested that a railway should run from Kells to Cavan; this was first suggested by the Railway Commissioners in 1838, but the project did not materialize, for it failed to gain approval. On 15 August 1846 the government decided that the relief committees should cease operating and that all relief works should stop at the same time in order to release workers for the harvest. The work of the relief committees helped the starving in the spring and summer of 1846. Indian meal was distributed. There was further catastrophe, for the new crop had failed. This occurred in the first fortnight of July 1846, and by August it was reported that the entire crop was lost in County Cavan. *The Anglo-Celt* reported as early as July that there was a great failure in the potato crop. Within a few weeks everything was back to square one.

The potato famine made a fearful impact in the neighbourhood of Cootehill. The small farmers were alarmed, and panic set in amongst the labourers in September. They marched on the houses of the landlords, demanding work and threatening to steal. The price of potatoes rocketed from sixpence per stone in May to one shilling in December; by January 1847 there were no potatoes available. In the winter, oatmeal cost twenty-four shillings per hundredweight, at a time when a labourer's wage was ten pence per day or five shillings per week. There were also reports of activities on the black market by smaller retailers and millers. They created a shortage in order to be able to increase prices. The Killeshandra oatmeal was bought for £20 per ton, and made 180 per cent profit. Indian meal was much cheaper and a ton of it would last as long as a half-ton of oatmeal. The Reverend J. J. Martine of Killeshandra requested the government to intervene and set up a depot in the area to supply them with fifty tons weekly at a reasonable profit. The local providers were not able to meet demand, and this caused famine.

Darkness reigned over Ireland, reaching high society. This was manifested at a regatta on 9 September. The Marquess of Headford said that he could think of nothing but starving labourers. Colonel Saunderson of Castle Saunderson, who lived near Belturbet, wrote that in County Cavan on 8 September an awful calamity seemed to be hovering over the Gaels. There was no useful employment, and roadworks were in a backward state, so relief could not easily meet the starving. Matthew McQuaid, the parish priest of Kilsherdany, near Cootehill, said that the workers were destitute and on the verge of starvation. The small farmers could only obtain a small amount of food and he recommended that useful employment be found at once.

Extraordinary sessions were held in the eight baronies in the last week of September 1846, and they voted a further £60 for relief. Delays in getting the public works off the ground, due to the fact that each project had to be brought before the Board of Works, caused great distress. Implementation was in the hands of two Board of Works engineers and district relief committees. In County Cavan there were fifteen such relief committees by October and local relief committees continued to function. By the end of October, 2,000 labourers were busy on the roadworks over the county; 9,000 by the middle of November; and by February 1847 the number had risen to 25,000 on about 4,000 schemes.

During the winter of 1846/7 there were a number of shortcomings. They were slow to start and they only made up ten per cent of the workforce. The wages were low (an average of four shillings per week, or

45

just enough to buy stores of oatmeal), and often not paid on time. There was a riot in Cavan town on the Saturday before Christmas 1846, when word came about that no wages would be paid that day. Complaints were made that there were too many overseers with nothing much to do. George Shaw, an agent of the Ballyhaise estate of Mr Humphrey, said that the qualifications for an overseer were a good frieze coat, a strong hay rope to bind around his waist and the sheltered side of a sunny bush for his books. There were reports of alleged favouritism in the awarding of works. At the Upper Loughtee Presentment Sessions on 14 December, Father Charles O'Reilly enquired of Lord Farnham if it was right that the people from Cavan and Denn, who were well off, should be employed in Lavey while many of his parishioners were near starvation.

On 20 March 1847 a command from the Board of Works dismissed twenty per cent of those employed in public works, and this paved the way for eventual closure. About twenty per cent were put out of work – a major decision for the authorities. At one scheme in Kilnaleck lots were drawn, and the report said that the wretched creatures on whom the lots fell raised a cry that still rang in his ears. It was like a sentence of death upon them. At Ballinagh, 406 men and children, who were employed breaking stones, were dismissed. In Ballymachugh one man was dismissed for attempting suicide, and another who lost his job became insane and murdered his wife. By mid-June the numbers employed in public works had fallen to a little over 2,000, and soon afterwards the works ceased. The spring crop was coming, and the small farmers who had been relieved for the season found themselves with little to do. They could buy seed, and about one tenth of the potato crop was sown. However, soup kitchens were introduced, and the local relief committee, established in the autumn of 1846, continued to function. They raised subscriptions for soup kitchens where the soup was free or at a small cost to the poor.

From time to time these committees acknowledged the help given to them from outside sources. The Society of Friends helped; John McDowel, a Cavan man living in Liverpool and later a member of the British Association, gave help; but in the main help came from local sources.

Mr Foster, agent for the Society of Friends, visited Cavan on 4 and 6 April 1847. He acknowledged the need for clothing as well as food. Grants of food and clothing from the Society of Friends were acknowledged in *The Anglo-Celt* in July and August 1847. Also involved were the infirmaries at Strabane, Ballyjamesduff and Cavan: their grants saved many lives.

The Temporary Relief Act was passed in Parliament in March 1847; this was also known as the Soup Kitchen Act. It reorganized relief committees, whose finances would be controlled by the Poor Law Union, and it authorized the local relief committees to issue rations free of charge. The cost would be partially met by local contributions, but mainly by a government grant repayable through the poor rate. The Soup Kitchen Act limited relief of poverty to the poor rate at a time when the Poor Law Unions in County Cavan were heavily in debt. They were reluctant to strike a new rate while some of the standing rate was owed. Food depots or soup kitchens were established throughout the county by the end of April. The Irish Relief Association had swung into action. Supplies of oatmeal and bread were asked for. Bakers produced cheap bread and bakeries were established by private enterprise in some areas. In June about one third of the population of each elected division was in receipt of rations. In the various other divisions – for example, in the Bailieborough Union, 16,000 were fed; in Tullyvin and the Ashfield division of the Cootehill Union, 5,200 out of a total population of 10,000 were fed and out of these 2,660 were cottiers owning an acre of land. During the five months of the Act's operation, the Bailieborough Union spend £12,400, of which £5,000 was paid to the government. The remaining £7,400 had to be repaid by the union from the poor rate. Thirty-five per cent of the population were receiving help from April to September 1847. The soup kitchens ceased operation in the same year. They had saved the lives of thousands.

Starvation to some extent had been kept at bay, but in the workhouses a new terror struck, manifesting itself as fever. In February 1847 there were 200 cases in the Cavan workhouse, where there was already an overcrowding problem. The fever was next heard of at Belturbet. By April the epidemic was widespread in County Cavan. It to some extent disappeared during July, but reappeared in the following winter and throughout most of 1848. The suffering from the fever had an effect upon Ulster. Typhus, relapsing fever and dysentery were the main perils and of those, it was dysentery that caused the most damage in the spring of 1847 due to poor diet. Doctors at Cavan town said that about one fifth of the population caught fever and that the mortality rate, which was under five per cent in the poorer classes, was sixty per cent among the upper classes. This shows that the famine was no respecter of persons. More people died from disease in Cavan during the famine than from starvation. Children were very vulnerable. An article about Cavan town in the *Dublin Journal of Medical Science* for the period February to May 1849 stated that there were 1,236 cases of fever attended to within the town and in a mile's radius of it. Eight funerals a day were reported to Maybolgie cemetery near Bailieborough. The rate of deaths in the workhouse was alarming. For the year ending 30 November 1847, 633 deaths were recorded in the Cavan workhouse. The worst period was April to June, during which time there were 240 deaths out of a population of 1,500, or an average of sixteen percent.

Dr Halpirn and Dr Mease made a thorough inspection of Cavan town and reported on 22 April 1847 that they had visited every house there. There were many cases of fever, twenty-five of dysentery, six of dropsy and six of other ailments. People were sleeping rough, and other little townlands were in a poor state. There was very little straw and other bedding, clothes were dirty, dung was heaped at the doors.

The fever hospital at Keadew, near Cavan, was overcrowded in May, and people were being turned away for lack of accommodation. A temporary hospital was set up in April to provide extra room in the workhouse. The hovels of the poor around Cavan were whitewashed. Fresh straw was supplied for bedding. The poor were carried from the country, where they had been living by the roadside, to be treated by the local health board in Cavan town.

An eight-year-old girl, Ann Magee was abandoned. She lived in a ditch for several days, and died of fever on 20 May in the fever huts. Dr Flemming reported from Bailieborough in May that dysentery or fever was rampant in the hovels of the area. Temporary fever hospitals were set up throughout the county in order to cope with the epidemic. A temporary fever hospital was set up by Dr Wade in Belturbet, and it had seventy-seven patients by 3 July; Virginia Fever Hospital had seventy-six paupers; and Cootehill had sixty at the same time. There were also hospitals opened in Ballyhaise (July), Ballyjamesduff (September), Kingscourt (October), and Shercock (December).

There were many more that could not make it to the hospitals. Most of them were buried in the ditches.

Most of the temporary establishments closed in the summer of 1848, but now a new epidemic swept through Cavan workhouse. There was opposition to the setting-up of a fever hospital for the local people, as an account in *The Anglo-Celt* reported in early July 1847. Stricken victims were seen in the neighbourhood of the town. The relief committee at first tried to erect fever sheds and to establish a board of health, but the inhabitants were not too keen on the idea. The temporary fever hospital was opened in April 1847 by Dr Wade in Belturbet. It was burned down, but eventually reopened in June. Nurses, doctors and clergy also fell victim to the fever. Patrick O'Reilly, chaplain to the Cavan workhouse, caught the fever, and died on 12 April 1847. On the same day James Smith of Cootehill died. A month later Father Francis McKiernan perished from the fever in Cavan. Another Catholic priest, chaplain to Cavan jail, died of fever. The Reverend Charles Beresford, Rector of Bailieborough, an active relief worker, also died. The doctors of other townlands also fell victim to the fever. Mrs Mitchell, matron of the Cavan workhouse, died; and so did Mr Gormley, master of the Cootehill workhouse.

The potato crop of 1847 was not affected by blight. The number of potatoes planted was on a par with previously years. Public works were abandoned, the soup kitchens abolished and the relief of distress was under the sole responsibility of the Poor Law guardians and the workhouse under the Poor Law Extension Act of 1847. If the workhouse was full, outdoor relief was obtainable.

Able-bodied men did not qualify for relief under the Poor Law Commissioners at the instigation of the boards of guardians. The sanction of outdoor relief was by use of officers. It was to be financed from the poor rates.

The Poor Law guardians were now faced with a problem: the workhouse at Cavan was already overcrowded and deeply in debt, with much of the previous rate still outstanding. It had one hundred paupers over capacity; it owed the sum of £4,500, but only £1,500 had been gathered. The guardians were reluctant to shoulder the total responsibility for relief of distress assigned to them. It was a great burden for them, so the Cavan board of guardians was dissolved in November and two guardians appointed. The guardians still administered the affairs of the Cavan board of guardians from December 1847 until March 1848. Cootehill was also in debt to the tune of £2,350, with much of the previous years' rate outstanding. The workhouse was full. However, efforts were made to make the act workable. Relief officers were appointed and they began to administer relief in December. Extra workhouse room was rented. The total population of the accommodation in the union was 1,150 in January 1848. There were complaints of failure by the guardians to relieve the famine at Ashfield, Larah and Kill. This culminated in the disbandment of the Cavan board of guardians and the Bailieborough board of guardians. The boards of guardians implemented the Act after a delay. Distress was mapped out, relieving officers appointed, depots hired, and supplies made available. A rate of between four shillings and one shilling in the pound was struck.

It was now, with the Poor Law Extension Act, that the able-bodied were able to obtain relief only in the workhouse. The workhouse was extended by renting houses throughout the union. In November 1848 the total housing for paupers in the Cavan Union was 3,000, including 1,300 in the original workhouse. There were 120 in the new fever hospitals and 1,620 in the houses at Killeshandra, Kildallan, Drumalee (Belturbet) and Sweelam, near Cavan. In mid-June 1849, six months later, the highest count of the poor in the Cavan workhouse was 3,734 paupers, including 1,955 children and 1,657 adults. Similar changes were made in the Cootehill Union, providing an extra 690 places; and in the Bailieborough Union 650 extra places were provided in ancillary workhouses. By January 1848 relieving officers were appointed and relief depots set up throughout Cavan county. Outdoor relief was supposed to be eight pence per week for adults and four pence for children. Indian meal was provided – 7lb per adult and 3½lb per child. In March 1848 the Cavan Union was providing half the relief for 9,000 paupers, and 700–800 were receiving relief until August. Then the numbers were cut to 6,000, and in September to 1,500 persons. In the Cootehill Union the number was about 6,000, which was reduced to 876 in September. There was also another workhouse in Cavan: 991 paupers were admitted to it in 1845 and 2,366 in 1851.

In March 1848 *The Anglo-Celt* criticized the rigid, inhumane Poor Law Extension Act.

A father, mother and eight children from the Cootehill area headed for Scotland in October 1847. The mother and seven of her children returned to Ireland in December and entered the Cootehill workhouse. In February 1848 she was told that she was a deserted wife and that she had to vacate the workhouse. She was told she would be eligible for outdoor relief provided that she signed an affidavit that she had been deserted by her husband. She refused and she was forced out. Two of her children died of starvation. The rest were saved by the generosity of the local parish priest, Father Matthew McQuaid, and the wife of the local minister. Another consequence of the Act was the process through which it brought pressure on the Poor Law. By July the rate struck varied from 4s. 6d. to 3s. in the Cavan and Cootehill unions to 7s. in the Bailieborough Union. This, combined with the inability of the poor to pay rent during the famine and the enforcement of the clause in the Poor Law Extension Act, stopped relief to anyone with a rood of land. The pressure was on the landlords, who had to pay the rates of tenants holding land valued at less than £4. They were obliged to clear such tenants off their estates so that they could qualify for outdoor relief. The landlords had cabins levelled so that no other paupers could occupy them.

John Kelly, a rate collector in the Milltown area outside Belturbet, wrote in the *Freeman's Journal* on 25 July 1848 that in the townland of

Coragh there were thirty tenants, of whom three were in jail for arrears of rent. Nine were dispossessed and their homes levelled. Their food would only last for two days. In August 1848 the Reverend Farrelly of Crossbane, Mullagh, wrote an open letter to absentee landlords. He said that it was impossible for landlords to expect rents while the tenants were reduced to the necessity of loading turf to Navan, nineteen miles away. They sold the turf for eight pence, of which one penny was spent on bread and half a stone of Indian meal. This was brought home to their families, some of which were made up of eight persons. He further said that it was necessary to look at providing several pounds of meal for eight persons in twenty-four hours, to relieve the distress of the tenants.

There were reports of eviction throughout 1848 and 1849, but no accurate statistics are available. Letters from three areas are worth looking at, as they paint a vivid picture of the inhumanity of the landlords and the disasters caused by estate clearances. The first letter was from Tom Brady, who lived near Cootehill, to the *Freeman's Journal* on 1 March 1848. In it he claimed that there were fifty vacant farms and 200 human beings set adrift on the land in bad weather. There was great fever and two children lay dead. Corpses lay by the highways, and the landlords had no pity. Common humanity was wanting. The landlords deprived the tenants of whatever crops were available, and they were prevented from obtaining outdoor relief.

On 29 December Father Foy in the parish of Shercock wrote to the *Freeman's Journal* in answer to an accusation by Lord Farnham that some Catholic priests were encouraging disobedience. He said that it was difficult to teach patience and virtue to those who saw their loved ones dying of fever, lying by the roadside – fathers, mothers, wives and children. They were driven from their homes into the bogs and ditches to meet starvation and death.

The last letter was from Matthew McQuaid of Kilsherdany on 19 January 1849. He wrote that there was never a more terrible campaign carried out against the poor than at present. There was rivalry amongst the agents over who could banish the most paupers. There had been three years of unmitigated famine. Everyone knew that the mere Irish were being banished from some estates and Protestants substituted for those on long leases.

At Cavan starvation and eviction continued throughout 1849. In June 1849, James Brown, Catholic bishop of Kilmore, addressed a congregation in Cavan town on the poor condition of some of the tenants, who were experiencing the fourth year of famine: they lay destitute of all means of supporting life. He also spoke about the inhabitants of Cavan town who were ashamed of their condition, with the prospect of starvation facing them. A charitable relief committee was established in the town. It helped 128 families, or 751 people, and provided them with Indian meal. Conditions were like those at Belturbet, Cootehill, Bailieborough and Killeshandra.

Many were set adrift by estate clearances – some perished, others ended up in the workhouse, some emigrated (but many would have lacked the means to do so), and others took to begging. In April 1848 *The Anglo-Celt* reported the evils of begging in the town and there was a daily influx of paupers into Cavan from the countryside.

The Anglo-Celt called for the enforcement of the Vagrancy Act. It addressed the topic in June, describing Mudwall Row in Cavan as a house of vice, pestilence and starvation. A number of cases were heard under the Vagrancy Act. Four small children, trained by their father and sister, walked the streets for two months, crying out for food. They were admitted to the workhouse and the father was given three months hard labour. In May a man named Mulligan from Cootehill stole a chicken and was lodged in Cavan Jail, where he died of starvation the following day. A report stated that many parents of destitute children had hidden inside roofless walls, and cried out for food. At the assizes there were many cases heard of stealing food and of murder or attempted murder against people protecting their property against the destitute and starving.

During the period of the famine the population of the county decreased from 243,000 in 1841 to 174,000 in 1851 – a reduction of 28.5%. The decline manifested itself from parish to parish, but within each parish certain townlands experienced an increase in population. The decline was greatest in East and Mid-Cavan. Here the parishes experienced a marked decline in population – Cootehill, 31.6%; Inniskeen, 36%; Kilsherdany, 36%; Knockbride, 33.5%; Mullagh, 33%; Drung, 32%; and Drumlane, 35%. In the west of County Cavan the percentage was much lower – Templeport, 19%; Kinawley, 14%; Kildallan, 23.7%; and Killinagh, 21%. In the west of County Cavan, where there was a smaller population than in the east, the Gaels had to take to the rough ground. Here they eked out an existence by growing small potatoes and oats. Here the decline was much slower. A much greater workforce had depended on the linen business to supplement their incomes, but the decline in this business also aggravated the conditions in the workhouses, which were struggling to cope with people arriving from the land.

It is difficult to determine how many died and how many emigrated.

Passengers were assisted to emigrate to the New World, but the Catholic Church was opposed to this. One Scott of Fort Frederick, Virginia, assisted people to emigrate in 1847. In November and December 1848 about sixty female paupers from the Cavan workhouse had their fares paid to emigrate by the union. Reports in the *Freeman's Journal* in 1848 said that people were finding it hard to obtain money to emigrate. The *Freeman's Journal* also featured an article from Kells on 25 October 1849 which reported the daily passage of the starving from Cavan town on their way to Drogheda and Dublin. For those who were able to raise the fare, emigration must have seemed an attractive choice, when the alternative was to die from famine in County Cavan.

Chapter 4

The Great Hunger in County Donegal

County Donegal is one of the largest as well as the wildest and most mountainous of Irish counties, but there is also much cultivatable soil. County Donegal had a population of nearly 30,000 persons, and more than two thirds were involved in agriculture, thinly spread over an area of 1,900,000 acres, of which little more than one third was reclaimed and cultivated. This is how James Hack of the Society of Friends found Donegal when he visited it late in the 1840s to investigate reports of the distress in the county.

A Royal Commission, eleven years earlier, had attempted to gain some insight into the extent of poverty in Ireland. Its findings in relation to Ballyshannon were founded on statements taken from the local clergy and landlords. The Reverend Francis McDonnell, PP reported that widows with children were sometimes assisted by small farmers, allowing them to build hovels on the outskirts of the bogs and on the sides of public roads. There were about 400 labourers in the region, of whom one hundred were in constant employment. Wages varied from eight pence per day to one shilling. Their diet consisted of potatoes, herrings, salt, stirabout and milk. Their clothing was meagre, filthy and wretched. Most labourers had to pay rent, varying from £2 to £3 per annum for a cabin and a few potatoes. The furniture in the hovels was pitiful, as was the bedding. The interior was smoky, from the fire that was lit upon the earth floor. The Reverend J. Cummins said that he was aware of about sixty cases of two families in one cabin.

Ballyshannon was prosperous in comparison to other parts of County Donegal. It was part of the Connolly estate, which comprised twenty-six townlands in the south-west of Donegal. Between 1830 and 1844

Edward Connolly spent £21,000 on improving agriculture on his lands. He introduced the rundale system and encouraged the enclosure of open fields and the setting-up of separate holdings. He gave grants for the building of houses. When tenants were placed on moorlands they were only charged a nominal rent for the first three years. Farm sizes varied from thee acres to 150 acres. There was, therefore, no efficient local agricultural industry in the region. Considerable quantities of wheat, grain and potatoes were exported from Ballyshannon and were valued at £11,000.

We now turn to the parish of Glencolumbkille during the first half of the nineteenth century. It was typical of many Donegal regions – wild and impoverished. The Reverend John Ewing, the Church of Ireland rector, described the parish in 1834. He said there was not one tree in the parish, and there were no wooden buildings nor good roads. Fish were available in the rivers, and of course there were some potatoes in the fields. By July 1844, when the Devon Commission sat in Donegal town, there was great pressure on the land in Glencolumbkille, and rents were ten times the average in County Donegal. The agent, William Hume, paid only £108 to Colonel Connolly for several thousand acres. James McCunningham of Farran MacBride, who reproached the tenant farmers of the parish of Glencolumbkille, said that he was paid £21 rent for twenty acres. He said that there was no mention of cow or calf in the countryside.

On 31 July 1838 the Act for more relief of the destitute poor in Ireland had passed into law. Poor Law Unions were set up in Donegal and workhouses were built. Outdoor relief was permitted, but it was severely limited in its capacity to cope with the disease throughout the island. John Mitchell expressed the contemporary attitude to the workhouse when he saw the Glenties workhouse in 1845. There was a new building and it was also the greatest, rearing its gables and pinnacles.

The Poor Law workhouse did little to relieve poverty before 1845 as most people felt the stigma of entering the building. In 1846 the workhouse struggled to cope with the crisis. The potato disease was spreading throughout the county and its effects were felt in the minutes of the meetings of the guardians of the respective workhouses. By January 1846 the Inishowen workhouse adopted the policy, since there were high prices for potatoes, that meal should be substituted until further orders: eight ounces for dinner to adults, and less for the others. The Letterkenny guardians felt obliged to point out the want of potatoes and the necessity of substituting meal – this was by mid-July 1846.

The Glenties Union found itself in a perilous position as the famine crept upon the land. The workhouse itself was not opened to receive the poor until May 1846. By November 1845, the guardians had met with Mr G. C. Otway, an assistant Poor Law Commissioner. He had voiced fears about being able to cope with the emergency which was gradually unfolding. The guardians of the Glenties Union were now anxious to open the workhouse.

Within a matter of weeks of its eventual opening, the implications of the famine were becoming apparent in the union. In July the master was directed to strike off his previous account for 60lb of potatoes as they were unfit to eat. By August the guardians sought to communicate with the Relief Commission on the necessity of receiving large quantities of Indian meal in the areas of Teelin, Killybegs, Portnoo and Rutland. If relief was not provided in a hurry, catastrophe was inevitable.

James Hack Tuke undertook a fact-finding mission in County Donegal in the late autumn of 1846, and he described the misery that everywhere prevailed. Many families were living on a single meal of cabbage, or even on a little seaweed. In Dunfanaghy he condemned the lack of development in the fishing industry and he left some meal for the poor. There was also a little turf, without which, in the bad weather, they would have been frozen to death. However, Dunfanaghy fared better than other areas during the critical winter of 1846/7. This transpired because the gentry on the local relief committees, led by Lord George Hill, defied the law and sold Indian meal below the going price. This prevented the fatal delays which had occurred in other areas.

The effectiveness of the Poor Law system was sporadic, according to Tuke's visits to workhouses. Only at Dunfanaghy, Milford and Stranorlar did the workhouses provide reasonable living conditions. At Dunfanaghy Tuke recorded that the workhouse was in adequate order and that the inmates were in good health. This was only a small workhouse, the number of inmates being 116. The Milford workhouse appeared in good order and the inmates in good health. There were one hundred admissions during the past week. The Stranorlar workhouse contained 388 inmates. They were also in good health, in pleasing contrast to many other establishments.

At Glenties, Ballyshannon and Letterkenny, conditions in the workhouses were substandard. Tuke visited the workhouse at Glenties, which was in a terrible state. The people were half starved and only half clothed. They had but one meal of oatmeal and water each day and at the time of his visit there was not sufficient for another day's supply. Some people were leaving the workhouse, but many preferred to sleep rough than to live in the hovels. At Letterkenny the diet consisted entirely of Indian meal. Tuke found that one fourth of the inmates were in the infirmary, and a large number of them were children. The children suffered great pain from what one member called epidemic cancer in the mouth, which had broken out suddenly. At Ballyshannon Tuke found the workhouse in bad condition. There were about 500 paupers, and the death rate was high. Two corpses were carried to the graveyard in an open cart without a ceremony or a procession of any kind.

The parish of Glencolumbkille, in the Glenties Union, was too remote for Tuke's party. When they were informed about the poverty in the region they sent a relief ship to Killybegs. According to tradition, in the parish of Glencolumbkille only one person died of the famine, but the evidence suggests otherwise. Glencolumbkille was remote and its landlords lived elsewhere. Colonel Connolly of Ballyshannon left his Glencolumbkille estate in the hands of his agents, the Humes of the Glen. There was also the notorious Alexander Hamilton, and stories of evictions on his lands have been passed down to us. Many paupers who could not pay their rent promptly were evicted from his lands.

The disparity in the numbers of people who sought refuge at different times in Donegal's workhouses is an indication of the regional impact of the effects of the famine on the people. Early in January 1847, while Ballyshannon had reached its accommodation limit, the Dunfanaghy, Donegal, Glenties and Inishowen workhouses all reported pressure on their resources. However, within a few weeks large numbers left the Glenties workhouse. In April the guardians, in response to typhus amongst the inmates, did not admit more paupers. About ninety people were in the workhouse, and the master was directed to admit up to 650. There was a general cessation of relief work, so the guardians were warned reluctantly not to admit more people. In May 1847 the poor rate of the Glenties Union rose from sixpence to fifteen shillings in the pound in order to cope with the numbers dependent upon relief, inside or outside the workhouse. Elsewhere demands were not so pressing. John Vandeleur Stewart, chairman of the Letterkenny guardians, blamed the Glenties situation partly on management problems, and partly on the ratio between resident and non-resident landlords. He wished to account for the fact that Glenties received 4,535 poor and Dunfanaghy received only 2,668. They said that the Poor Law was administered by the guardians, who were carefully selected.

Evidence now started to accumulate of the extent of the destitution within the county. This was presented to the Belfast Ladies' Association for the Relief of Irish Destitution, one of the many charitable associations which sprang up in response to the troubled winter of 1846/7. Barry D.

Hewetson, writing to the association in February described the effects on the population. In one house he found a family of fourteen. There was no fire in the house. People were cold and there were many deaths, including children. He said that Lord George Hill was doing all that he could. He was busy from morning to night.

Reports from Arranmore, Carrigart, Templecrone and Glencolumbkille said that the winter of 1846/7 was the bleakest. The Reverend Henry Carne, writing from Killybegs in January 1847, thanked the committee for their generous grants, which enabled him not only to feed the hungry but also to obtain useful employment for the peasants.

In June 1845, twenty-five per cent of children at Glencolumbkille were in receipt of relief from the British Relief Association, which administered relief in schools. This prompted an increase of children in the schools. Captain O'Neill, who visited the region for the Relief Commissioners, reported that the numbers pressing for admission to the schoolhouse were great. But he had not as yet brought about relief. He was obsessed with bureaucratic detail – typical of the period. There was a dread of allowing money to be spent on anyone who was undeserving. This caused many delays. The parish of Glencolumbkille lost seventeen per cent of its population as a result of the Great Hunger – through disease, starvation and emigration.

Like conditions prevailed in the Rosses, where the population was 10,000. Prosperity was hardly heard of in the west of Donegal. Food had to be brought to the starving by ship. The ships had to anchor in adverse conditions and to distribute food. Rathmullan, Downings, Rutland Harbour and Killybegs were important landing places. Now came Indian meal, rice and biscuits brought to Rutland Harbour in government ships and later ferried across to Burtonpoint in rowing boats. The food was distributed by police and other personnel. Dr George Frazer Brady volunteered his service. A young girl called Sally Niece nursed the sick for the sum of 4s. 6d. per week.

The plight of the islanders of Arranmore was described by an American visitor, who visited the island in 1847: No one had a morsel of food; they ate bits of turnips and seaweed. Shellfish were a luxury. They did not ask for charity. The Inishowen Union, in the north of Donegal, which had a population of 43,569 and which was served by the Carndonagh workhouse was amongst the first to be affected by the potato disease. In the autumn of 1845 the crop was almost totally destroyed in many areas. By the end of 1845 relief committees were raising subscriptions which were matched by the government. In February 1846 a Presbyterian minister, John Mackey, reported that 3,400 souls in the parish of Upper Fahan were in great distress, but the workhouse was already full. In May the clergy of the parish of Donagh wrote to the Poor Law Commissioners telling them the numbers that were likely to experience great suffering in the summer if relief was not obtained. It was estimated that the casualties would be 165–181 Anglicans, 120 Presbyterians, and 140 Roman Catholics.

Ballyshannon, in the most southerly part of Donegal, had been largely unaffected by the famine in 1845. However, in 1846 the *Ballyshannon Herald* observed that the weather continued to be fine, and the potato blight had started to spread. Indian meal, as elsewhere, was now resorted to. Some merchants had brought it from Sligo, and this prevented hundreds from dying of starvation. Workhouses were well equipped for the impending tragedy. On 12 September 1846, the Poor Law Commissioners called the attention of the boards of guardians to the increase of poverty and suffering due to the failure of the potato crop. They begged that relief would be made available. They also wanted suitable accommodation (if the workhouse could afford it) over a considerable length of time.

Around this time there were about 125 paupers in the Ballyshannon workhouse, but it had been built to house 500 inmates. By November the number stood at 500 inmates. The cost of keeping a pauper had risen from four pence farthing a week. The guardians now decided not to make any more admissions to the workhouse, but by 5 December 1846 the number of inmates was 501, rising to 596 by 27 March 1847. During the summer of 1847 the numbers fell temporarily. Soup kitchens provided relief and soon there were vacancies for 200 paupers in the workhouse. The guardians then ruled that there should not be any more outdoor relief. By 30 October the master of the workhouse told the board that there was no more accommodation available, since numbers had risen to 540. If there were more applicants, what could be done?

By 27 November 1847 the number of inmates rose again to 561. On 1 January there were 769 inmates. By the following week the numbers stood at 626. Many elderly and infirm paupers took to sheltering in the workhouse at eight pence per week. The guardians refused admission to the poor of other unions. By 8 January 1848 the Poor Law Commissioners instructed that no paupers from any union were to be admitted to the workhouse. Before the failure of the crop, the workhouse diet was very frugal, but wholesome. Porridge, potatoes and buttermilk were served. When the potatoes became uneatable, Indian meal was served. It was not as nourishing as potatoes and the poor found it unpalatable. Early in 1847 the price of Indian meal rose from £18 to £27 per ton. There was also an increase in the price of oatmeal. The rise in price was in line with other countries in Europe. The price increase in Indian meal was principally due to profiteering by those involved in its transit and sale. The government bent under pressure. Indian meal imported by the government later in 1846 for distribution in the impoverished regions of the west was distributed at the recommendation of Trevelyan. It was held in storage until other sources of food had failed. The meal was bought at £13 per ton. For fear of undercutting prices charged by local merchants, the meal was sold at the government depots at £19 per ton at the end of December.

Supplies of meal became unobtainable at Ballyshannon, where the board of guardians applied to a Mr Hamilton to obtain meal for the workhouse. This was probably John Hamilton of St Ernan's who imported Indian meal and other foods into Donegal town for distribution amongst his tenants. Hamilton was deserted by James Hack Tuke, who was devoting his life to the service of the poor. Tuke found that at Ballyshannon the gentry, far from not caring about the plight of the poor, were pulling their weight for the welfare of the paupers. Colonel Connolly and family remained at their home for the winter in order to provide relief. The Society of Friends offered money in proportion to the amount raised in the town for the establishment of a soup kitchen. Colonel Connolly subscribed one third of the amount (£600) to the Ballyshannon Relief Committee. He reduced his Donegal rents by twenty-five per cent.

With the resumption of Indian meal as the staple food in the workhouse, the cost of keeping a pauper fell, but a committee of the board observed that there was great sickness amongst the children. It was proposed that each pauper be allowed a good and wholesome meal of rice and milk daily. Dr Kelly, medical officer of the workhouse, said that it was a good idea to remove children under twelve to a separate house. The welfare of the children improved and there was a reduction in dysentery. Dr Kelly blamed deaths from dysentery on the food of the house and the lack of clothing for working men in the inclement weather. The master said that he was obliged to take the men from their work due to the extreme cold that had affected their feet, as many were without shoes and stockings.

Pestilence followed starvation. In November 1846, the Ballyshannon guardians received a letter from the Poor Law Commissioners pointing out the danger of exceeding the limit of numbers in the workhouse. The board therefore did not admit any more paupers until the inmates were provided with clothing and shelter. The numbers had now risen from

184 to 469. The *Ballyshannon Herald* was alarmed at the spread of fever in the workhouse. On 2 April 1847 it was reported that the workhouse of the union was crowded to excess. This caused fever and dysentery to torment the inmates.

During July 1847 a temporary fever ward was built. It contained only fifty beds, although there had been one hundred fever cases by June. However, care of the poor went ahead despite the crisis. Disagreement amongst the masters of the union now became prominent. The relief committee was concerned with the question of finance and the controlling of temporary buildings, and the board provided financial support. On 4 November 1847, a prominent Ballyshannon doctor, a relative of another doctor, wrote to the Poor Law Commissioners to complain that the Ballyshannon guardians refused to pay the expenses of the temporary relief of the fever hospital. The commission found in favour of the relief committee. Deaths at Ballyshannon continued to rise in 1848, with thirteen dying from fever in the last week of January. Dr Stephens, one of the dispensing doctors, caught the fever of a patient, but he recovered. By this time the epidemic was on the wane. The number of deaths had fallen from sixty in February to thirteen in December.

At Inishowen, fever made an appearance in early 1846. The Moville Famine Relief Committee reported that the fever had set in, and in many cases it was fatal. Fever in the Carndonagh workhouse was reported in March 1847, with eight inmates affected. The guardians segregated the sick, but treatment was non-existent. The guardians were told to treat the patients by applying alcohol, but the record shows that only a bottle of wine was purchased.

Burial was a major problem. At the Ballyshannon workhouse the authorities recorded a crisis on 8 May 1847. The master reported that resistance had been offered to the interment of the dead at several burial grounds. There was an accumulation of dead bodies as the death rate rose. One inmate died of spotted fever, another of dysentery. Some of the dead remained from days before. It was decided to locate a pauper's graveyard at Mullaghnashee in the town. The record of the number of dead is not available for the Ballyshannon workshouse, as it is for other workhouses. The cost of coffins recorded in the minutes of the Ballyshannon board of guardians provides some idea of the numbers of dead, but it has been suggested that coffins were dispensed with. An Act had empowered the relief committees to make arrangements for decent burial of the poor. A record of payment by the Ballyshannon board of guardians of £13 15s. was half the amount demanded by Mr

Flanaghan for the many dead. Now burial would take place immediately after a person died of the fever. This indicates that the Ballyshannon workhouse had adopted a procedure permitted under the Act. Payment by the authorities for burials was usually per corpse, and according to oral tradition in Tipperary this was a shilling or so per body. The Ballyshannon guardians paid a similar rate. Records point out that approximately 550 burials took place.

There was a shortage of clean water and sanitation was inadequate for the increased numbers in the workhouse. By September 1847 the minutes mention an overflowing cesspool outside the women's yard, and in October it was ordered that further measures should be taken to deal with sanitation. The use of sewage as a fertilizer was permitted by workhouse regulations. In November, a Mr Darcy, the temporary inspector, complained to the commissioners that the sewers were creating a terrible stench and were most offensive. The problem persisted, and the master reported that the sewage was emptying into the water tank, so there was a shortage of clean water. In January 1848 the master reported that there was an inadequate supply of water in the well, and by the end of the month he reported that bedding and clothing had not been washed for three weeks due to the water shortage. The guardians ordered that two casks for carrying water from the river should be provided, at reasonable cost.

The funding of the workhouse was regarded by the government as the responsibility of the ratepayers, and any advance made from the government was given reluctantly on the understanding that it would be repaid. In September 1846 the commissioners recommended that the means of affording relief should be made available to the most generous extent. The guardians were obliged to make an increase in union rates above that struck in July to provide food for the paupers. There was great difficulty in raising the rate due to the great distress obtaining in the union. By January an appeal was made, asking the Lord Lieutenant to help with the upkeep of the Ballyshannon workhouse. Otherwise the paupers would have to struggle along by themselves. At the end of February 1847, the commissioners loaned £60 to the guardians, who expressed amazement at the small sum of money. Small sums continued to be paid weekly during the year until the commissioners refused, in July, to make any more advances. In March the Poor Law Commissioners agreed to lend £240 for paupers' clothing.

By June the Poor Law Commissioners urged the guardians to collect rates before the potato harvest and not to be dependent on the government. Collection of rates continued to be difficult. Rates were waived owing to the fact that the workhouses in question were 'down' and no longer taxed. A Mr Kitson was relieved of paying further rates in the division of Devenish. Eviction therefore took place on a considerable scale. An account of evictions in the Ballyshannon Union has been preserved in oral tradition. After an eviction the pauper's hovel was burnt down. After this the bailiff and his associates left the scene. The landlord was present at evictions and he offered the sum of £1 to anyone that would set light to the hovels. The thatch of the houses went up in flames, and it was made certain that the paupers could not reoccupy their houses. By 1847 the ratepayers violently resisted paying the rate. Mr Darcy reported that in the wild districts, where violence might loom, all the rate collections should be made with the assistance of the police. There was a feeling of insecurity abroad. Some of the ex-official guardians left the boardroom early. They did not wish to be out in the dark. Only a small proportion of the outstanding rates were collected.

The workhouse, however, maintained the provision of education and religion, as required by legislation. The Ballyshannon workhouse had two chaplains – one Catholic and one Protestant. The Protestant chaplain demanded an increase of his £20-per-annum salary because of the increase in his duties, which obliged him to keep a horse. There was an increase in the number of Protestants in the workhouse; and this was reflected in the purchase of six Bibles and catechisms for the use of Protestant children. Bread and wine for Holy Communion was paid out of workhouse funds for the Protestant inmates. In August 1847 an additional thirty prayer books were bought. For secular studies there was a schoolmaster and schoolmistress. The Superintendent of National Workhouse Schools reported on 16 January that the female teachers were well qualified to teach reading, spelling and sewing. The male teachers could teach reading, arithmetic and writing. The character of the books for learning was good. But the male schoolroom was equipped in the course of the year with only one desk and a set of tablets. The female school was furnished with twelve corporation spelling books.

The master of the workhouse earned £20; matron, £15; porter, £6; and there was also a clerk. The gate porter was an important fellow, and a sentry box was built for him. He was provided with a warm coat and a pair of shoes, to wear if he left the workhouse. It was rumoured that the workhouse master had made one female member pregnant. There was also conflict between master and matron. The Ballyshannon guardians and the Poor Law Commissioners investigated the allegations concerning the morality of the matron, Mrs Kennon. She was, however, dismissed for making false accusations, but the commissioners found that the investigation had been concluded in an illegal manner. There was an increase in rowdy behaviour in the workhouse due to overcrowding. Punishments ranged from confinement to withholding food. On one occasion boys threw stones at the assistant master. Corporal punishment was not against workhouse regulations.

Attempts were made in all the County Donegal workhouses to keep the inmates fit and employed. The boards of guardians throughout County Donegal received orders for sledgehammers, scrapers, picks and barrows. In the Ballyshannon workhouse each adult male was expected to break half a ton of stone per day. Women did the housework and spinning wheels were available. In addition the Poor Law relief committees were made up of many gentry and clergy. The earliest of these committees started to work in Inishowen following the failed potato crop in 1846. By the end of the year, local relief committees were raising subscriptions, which were matched by the government contributors. By that time the numbers of starving and destitute had increased dramatically, so the finance was inadequate. Only one fifth of those eligible were able to obtain employment. The wage was nine pence per day, and when funds ran out the roads were left in an impossible condition.

In 1847 the Moville Famine Relief Committee reflected the growing powerlessness of local committees to cope with the increasing scarcity of food. The Ballyshannon Relief Committee came into existence in October 1846. The aim had been to solicit donations and sell meat at cut prices. There was a store at College Street. Large sums of money were available to provide meal, which was sold in November 1846 to the poor. Public works were proposed by a presentment session held in September 1846. However, they were surrounded by bureaucratic delays and inclement weather. The relief committee was dismayed by the condition of the paupers. The severity of weather and the deep fall of snow added greatly to the suffering of the poor. The poor souls at work on the roads, almost all of whom were women, were clothed in miserable rags, unfit for exposure to the cold. There were delays in paying wages and this caused further hardship.

On arrival at Ballyshannon, Tuke reported that he had again heard complaints that the men employed on public works were badly paid. They had not received any pay for up to ten days. The money was sitting in the bank. Oral tradition tells us of the appalling conditions in Donegal. Relief was slow in coming owing to the primitive methods of transportation, and the long distance from Dublin, from where relief was directed. Money was also sent to pay the men on relief work, who were mainly involved in road-making.

In January 1847 the Temporary Relief Destitute Persons Ireland Act, sometimes known as the Soup Kitchen Act, came into force. The distribution of meal and soup was in the hands of relief committees. There was an appeal from Clonmany Relief Committee to provide cheap meal for the destitute. The soup kitchens went ahead, providing thin gruel for the starving. But in August the Poor Law Commissioners, assuming that the blight had ended, began to look forward to a reduction of the numbers in the workhouses. After this all relief was channelled through the newly amended Poor Law.

Large numbers emigrated from County Donegal, mainly to America and Canada. They sailed from ports such as Londonderry, Sligo and Donegal town. A government scheme was called into existence by the Colonial Secretary, Earl Grey, to send orphans to Australia. In Ballyshannon sixteen female orphans were chosen to emigrate to Australia. Lieutenant Henry, the Emigration Commissioner's agent, visited the Ballyshannon workhouse and chose sixteen orphan girls between fourteen and eighteen. Each girl was equipped with two flannel petticoats, six pairs of socks, two pairs of shoes and two gowns. It was estimated that it would cost £5 per head to equip the girls. They were to have free passage from Plymouth to Sydney. The orphans of Ballyshannon set out on their long journey from Ballyshannon to Plymouth under the leadership of the assistant master of the Ballyshannon workhouse. On Monday, 30 October 1848, the sixteen girls set sail from Plymouth on board *The Inchinan* in the company of 148 orphan girls from other Irish workhouses. They reached Sydney on 13 January 1849. The list of orphan emigrants included such names as Margaret Sweeney, Rose Reid, Margaret McBride, Sally Lennon and Biddy Smith. But the Earl Grey scheme was short-lived and terminated in 1850.

Dockside procedure for emigrants can be found in the diary of William Allingham, a Ballyshannon poet. He was appointed customs officer in Donegal town in 1846. He recorded the comings and goings of vessels, measurements of logs and deals and 'broad-stuff'. He saw to the fittings and provisions of emigrant ships, and when ready for sea the passengers came forward (men, women and children) to pay the doctor and himself.

During this period poets were preoccupied not with the disturbing details of the famine but with less worldly affairs. Poets wrote in beautiful English of love and romance and in relation to that all external things appeared trivial to them. William Allingham complained of suffering from anxiety, which arose out of his longing for culture, conservation and opportunity. He corresponded with Leigh Hunt, and in February 1847 he wrote that as well as food there was a supply of fuel. This is the only reference to the famine to be found in Allingham's writing of the period, apart from the chapter on a meeting at the Ballyshannon workhouse. In Allingham's letters and diary there is little intimation that he was living near to starvation and death. The Allingham family were involved in the relief committees set up during the famine.

Allingham is not alone in his lack of description of the famine. Chris Morash, in his introduction to *The Hungry Voice*, discusses the failure of so many Irish poets to find adequate expression for the experience of starvation. The native Gaelic tradition talked of various famines, but there was no such precedent in English literature. Famine forced the poets to make hard choices at the sight of so many of their fellow men being driven to the limits of existence. It took Allingham another thirteen years to find expression for the famine in his poem 'Lawrence Bloomfield'. This was a widely acclaimed indictment of landlord evictions.

Mary Anne Sheil, a Ballyshannon diarist, reported that the fever carried off all those who contracted it. She said there were disturbances locally on 21 April 1848, and great confusion in the town about the arresting of people who called themselves 'Ribbonmen'. Later, in July 1848, she reported that markets were well stocked, as were the jails. She did not know what had befallen the people and she prayed that things would get better. The unsettled condition of the countryside resulted in the billeting of British officers on her husband's home at Ballyshannon.

A breakdown in civilization was to be expected as a consequence of the great famine. In many quarters of Ireland serious cases arose both during and after the famine years. Donegal experienced some increase in crime, but this was on a relatively small scale. James Hack Tuke wrote that he had never witnessed such high morale, for the Irish had faith that the famine might shortly come to an end. He could not recall an instance of a peasant begging for food. As the winter of 1846/7 closed in, distress in the Ballyshannon Union was evident. A series of crimes were reported in the *Ballyshannon Herald*: two tons of meal were taken from the Abbey Mill and shipped across the Erne under cover of darkness. Several head of cow were also driven off. Meal was stolen from the Poor Law relief committee's meal store in College Lane. On Christmas Eve there was an act of piracy when bacon and ham were taken from a boat owned by a Mr Chism, a Ballyshannon merchant. Also reported was a poor-man's procession through Ballyshannon, led by a man carrying a loaf of bread.

The attempted collection of the Poor Rate from families who were destitute led to violence. By November 1847 the Poor Law inspector at

Ballyshannon sent a report saying that the poor had great difficulty in meeting their obligations. They were armed with sticks and scythes, and he narrowly escaped being killed. However, serious crime fell during 1846, and transportation to Australia fell too. In County Fermanagh, where the population was half that of Donegal, there were twenty-four instances in the transportation records in 1846. During 1847 Donegal was hit by a minor crime wave, and transportation sentences rose to thirty-one, for crimes of theft, larceny and receiving stolen goods. In the same year, 114 persons were sentenced in Fermanagh to transportation, and thirty-two persons received the same sentence in Donegal – once again for theft including the stealing of food and clothing. Allingham witnessed one of these sentences and recorded it in his diary for 29 December 1848: a girl was convicted of stealing a purse and was sentenced to seven years' transportation. She was removed crying out violently. It seemed a severe sentence.

The increase in transportation in County Donegal points to an increase in serious crime. The figures compare well with neighbouring counties, with the exception of County Sligo, which also had a low rate of transportation. The records show that for serious crime in 1849 transportation was the punishment. A number of severe sentences were imposed. The age of the 'criminals' ranged from sixteen to twenty years.

There are many roads remaining in County Donegal today, bearing such names as 'Brachan Road' or 'Line', which comes from an Irish word for soup. The experience of soup-taking is remembered, and also the term 'malebag' (meal bag). Accounts often relate how families came into prosperity. There are many paupers' graves, and in 1995, at Ballyshannon, a monument to those who had died was unveiled. The great iron boiling pots in which the soup and gruel was made may be seen at many locations in County Donegal. Donegal Historical Society has received a large gruel pot on permanent loan; it was previously kept at Coolmore House, Rossnowlagh (one of the homes of the unpopular landlord, Alexander Hamilton). During the famine the pot was used at Brachan Bray, the highest point in the neighbourhood. The site was chosen so that only those that had enough energy to climb the hill could be fed. The pot has now been placed on a site at the Franciscan friary at Rossnowlagh, in memory of the dead. The Dunfanaghy workhouse has been restored as a museum and heritage centre. At Ballyshannon plans have been made to restore one wing of the workhouse, which has been well preserved since the 1850s. Those dreaded buildings should surely continue to stand as a memory of the suffering of the Irish over 150 years ago.

Chapter 5

The Great Hunger in County Down

The eastern divisions of County Down fared badly as a result of the famine. Reports of suffering in Belfast were not less distressing than in the rest of Ireland. This was the opinion of the *Banner of Ulster* in February 1847. County Down was considered by contemporaries the most prosperous part of Ulster. Lord Londonderry (who owned much of North Down) did not like the idea of relief committees or grand juries sticking their noses into his affairs. Only three of Ireland's Poor Law Unions opted not to provide outdoor relief. Antrim, Belfast and Newtownards unions all wanted provisions. The Newtownards Union does not appear to have suffered. The Newtownards Union covered an area of about 54,000 acres and had a population in 1841 of 60,285. It was divided into electoral divisions – Newtownards, Mount Stewart, Greyabbey, Kircubbin, Ballywalter, Ballyhalbert, Carrodore, Bangor, Donaghadee, Comber, Ballygowan, Tullynakill, Ballymagluff, Kilmood and Moneyreagh.

The Londonderry clan was the greatest of the landowners. It granted a custom known as 'tenant right', and this was also the custom in other estates. Ten years before the famine, Lord Londonderry's agent claimed that the state of agriculture in the parish of Newtownards was rapidly improving. Farmers now used a five-course crop rotation. It was also recommended to apply cattle manure and lime. A few farms were of one hundred acres, though the average size of a farm was much less. In the Newtownards parish most farms were of ten to fourteen acres. In Loughriscouse the average farm was less than six acres. The better lands were able to provide fifteen hundredweight of wheat per acre – slightly above the national average. In 1844 there was an excess of labourers, and their condition was not improving.

Newtownards had been founded in the thirteenth century by the Normans and refounded at the time of the Ulster plantation in the seventeenth century. The *Parliamentary Gazetteer* of Ireland described it as one of the few towns that were of size and importance in County Down. It was one of the most attractive towns in the north of Ireland. The weaving of muslin in the town employed a large number of the male population. The embroidering of muslin, for the Glasgow manufacturers, employed the females.

By 1847 there were 600 looms at work and 1,000 women were busied with embroidery. Newtownards also served as a retail and merchant centre for North Down and the Ards Peninsula. Markets were held each Saturday and fairs four times a year. The town had a manor court, a court leet, petty sessions and quarter sessions. Behind the facade of the Market House – the largest of any provincial town in Ireland – lay unhealthy backstreets, small and crowded. The population almost doubled in the 1830s to a total of 7,621. In 1841 Market Street was described as being covered with dunghills. Ann Street also had many dunghills, and there were open sewers in most streets. Newtownards had no dispensary, and the Ordnance Survey of the 1830s said that help was essential, for the town's population was in a sickly condition. Fever was prevalent. The workhouse was built in 1841 to house 600; it contained on average about 200 paupers. Seven hundred females in the town depended upon their own skilled manual labour. There was, therefore, a sizable number of vulnerable folk in the town and in the parish of Newtownards in the mid-1840s.

By 1821 Newtownards and district had benefited considerably as a result of the exertions of the Londonderrys. The 3rd Marquess, however, was an absentee landlord. He was Charles William Stewart, the younger half-brother of Viscount Castlereagh. He had made a reputation for himself as a cavalry officer in the Napoleonic Wars and was ambassador to Vienna from 1814 to 1822. In 1819 he had married the wealthy Durham heiress, Frances Anne Tempest. Her father had considerable investments in property and coal mines in County Durham. Her mother was the Countess of Antrim. The couple were now the wealthiest in the British Isles. Lord Londonderry preferred to live in England, where he managed his English estates.

By the end of 1846 the potato crop in the area was, in the words of the Newtownards board of guardians, a total failure. However, quantities of potatoes were mainly exported to Scotland and England from Bangor, Donaghadee, Ballywalter, Kircubbin, Comber and Ardmillan. Due to the failure of the crops there were no exports in 1845 and 1846. There was not enough to feed the labourers in the Newtownards area. The *Northern Whig* reported that the labouring class in Newtownards were now abandoning the use of potatoes and resorting to an oatmeal diet. There was a five-fold increase in demand for oatmeal by the labourers, whose main diet had been potatoes. In Newtownards prices rose and the position of the labouring classes was determined by prevailing conditions. The situation became critical. With the absence of potatoes and the high prices of other foods, the farmers could not afford to feed the labourers. Extreme destitution prevailed and unemployment coincided with a rapid increase in the cost of living.

To ease matters many landlords in County Down reduced rents. William Sharman Crawford of Crawfordsburn published a letter to his tenants. He said that he would accept whatever rent his tenants could pay and he would inquire into the famine conditions. His letter was in contrast to one from Lord Londonderry to his agent, which was published on 17 November 1846 in the *Downpatrick Recorder*. He stated that landlords should be free to decide for themselves what rent should be payable. He was open to make concessions in severe conditions, but he was averse to sweeping rent reductions, which he said were dangerous and fatal. He said that he was afraid of the unrest of his own tenants. J. W. Maxwell allowed his tenants in the Groomsport and Downpatrick districts an abatement of fifteen per cent on rents in the year ending 1 November 1848. This was extended in the following year to twenty per cent.

Public works at Newtownards were organized mainly by voluntary contributions. Famine crept upon the weavers. Food rose in price, work all but disappeared, and the poor were forced to attend the workhouse. Oatmeal was 3s. 1d. and potatoes were 10d. Indian meal was bought to feed the poor. Men aged between fifteen and eighty worked outside in the bad weather, though many were infirm and weakened by hunger. Some died. When these schemes were completed, an unnamed local gentleman (who had an estate near Newtownards) employed a number of men for the same amount of money to do odd jobs on his property – but he was only able to help a small number of those seeking work. More fines were imposed and men were paid twopence per day to break stones on the North Street hill. This figure compares not unfavourably with the average rate of one penny per day, paid out of government-run public-works schemes.

The numbers entering the workhouse doubled between January and July 1847. In mid-December 1846 it exceeded 600. The workhouse had not been built to cope with such numbers. The guardians threatened to discharge single, fit paupers. They ordered the fumigation of newly built famine hospitals. They instructed the architects to draw up plans for additional living space; and carpenters were employed to build temporary beds in one of the boys' dormitories. The admission procedure was also tightened up. Admission was only available for those who were in bad health. It was placed on record that this measure was necessary to guard against overcrowding, which in turn would foster disease, especially amongst children.

Early in December 1846 Lady Londonderry arranged to have clothes distributed amongst the poor at her home at Mount Stewart. Lady Londonderry organized work at Mount Stewart at increased wages, and she also augmented the number of workers. She recommended that a soup kitchen be set up and financed by voluntary subscription. Lord Londonderry donated £20 and his wife £10. They then left for their house at Wynyard Park, County Dublin. On 21 December a public meeting at the Market House concluded that a soup kitchen was not the best means of relief. A deputation was sent to the guardians and this insisted that the numbers in the workhouse should not exceed its original purpose. The deputation consisted of the Reverend Townley Blackwood, parish minister; the Reverend Hugh Moore, minister of the Non-Subscribing Presbyterian Congregation; Major F. D. Montgomery of Regent House; and five merchants at Newtownards. These policies were a kind of outdoor relief. To many, outdoor relief seemed to encourage dependency and apathy. It had been prohibited by the 1838 Poor Law Act. This was a view held by other landlords, namely John Andrews and Robert Gordon of Florida Manor, Kilmood. There was stalling for time, and it was proposed that requests should be passed on to the Poor Law Commissioners, probably in full knowledge that they would be turned down. A majority carried out amendments that they thought were necessary, practicable and highly desirable, in view of the overcrowding in the workhouses.

An alarm was sounded by the guardians. They recorded in the minutes of 30 December that the board declared it right to complain about the overcrowded conditions in the workhouse. Female children slept three to a bed for want of space – and sometimes seven to a bed. A room might measure 17' x 14'. Many rooms were crowded and had low ceilings. Ventilation was poor. The nursery measured 30' x 40' and was often overcrowded. There were up to thirty nurses and forty children, and their mothers occasionally visited the children. The house was not free from diarrhoea, especially amongst the young. The board

71

concluded that increased sickness would be the result of overcrowding. Andrews was also becoming concerned. On 10 January 1847 he wrote to Lord Londonderry saying that matters were getting out of hand. The importation of food was not seeming to help matters. Prices went up; and the day-to-day suffering of the poor was getting worse. Families without breadwinners were particularly vulnerable. Their numbers were great in Newtownards. Visiting committees were appointed on the following Tuesday. The want of potatoes led to an increase of grain for the paupers, but supplies were limited on the open market and he said that there was also a want of money available for rent. He said that he and others had to do their best.

He wrote again on 18 January, and his letter sounded a note of alarm. He acknowledged the fact that the Newtownards area was in dire straits. The number of poor people was increasing. The condition of even the fully employed labourers was serious and others were also in serious difficulties. The small farmer had little to sell. Seedcorn had to be extracted from available stocks. Alarm was in the air. He said he did not know what would become of everyone if the weaving industry were to fail. There was no work in Newtownards for hundreds of hand-loom weavers. At Newtownards a subscription fund was started and a soup kitchen came into operation by the end of January 1847. Lord Londonderry had increased his contribution to £50 and his wife's had increased to £20. The *Northern Whig* of 6 February 1847 reported that it regretted the distress prevailing in the town of Newtownards. In order to alleviate matters, soup kitchens had been established and rations of soup and bread were dispensed from one o'clock until two o'clock to those who wanted to purchase. From two o'clock until three o'clock soup and bread were distributed to families who had been recommended by visiting committees for further relief. Many people took advantage of the soup-kitchen facilities. The committee published the names of subscribers to the fund which had been set up to offset the expenses of the soup kitchen. Lord Londonderry headed the subscription list with £50. Reference was also made to donations from businesses in Glasgow through their agents in Newtownards, particularly from Messrs S. R. R. J. Lewis (£25) and Charles Paul Ewing & Co. (£10).

The *Banner of Ulster* shed further light on the operation of the soup kitchens. It reported that they were exceedingly well managed, but confessed the fact that it was only after 200 families were issued with tickets that stability had been maintained. Those that did not have tickets or money obtained free soup. About 2,000 persons were fed from the soup kitchens and one hundred gallons of soup were given free each day. Some of the rural poor walked two miles into Newtownards each day to obtain relief. The *Newtownards Independent* recorded that a great number of poor folk gathered where soup was being distributed. They also required clothing items, such as shawls or old petticoats, as their clothing was not fit to be seen, even in a dog kennel. It was hard to obtain a glass of water. Females had insufficient clothes to cover them in their squalid wretchedness.

The soup kitchen stayed open until midnight. There were unruly scenes – jostling and fighting. On 2 February Andrews confided to Lord Londonderry that no great privation had been caused by the labouring classes. Several of the needy were badly situated and his plan was to press those who were destitute to sell up and emigrate. On 5 February he reported that the soup kitchen was much visited. He was aware that the destitute were pressing upon the workhouse, although it was unable to accommodate extra poor. Such people had little or no future in Ireland.

In Comber, private charity was addressing the lamentable state of affairs. In January 1847 some ladies set up a committee and sold meal and corn at reduced prices. Women and girls knitted and served. On 4 February, after a meeting, a soup kitchen was set up, and this was much visited. It supplied each day 230 families with free bread and soup. Another one hundred families had soup sold to them at one halfpenny per quart. The soup cost about £30 per month, of which Lord Londonderry contributed £10. These measures appeared to be effective. At Bangor, a soup kitchen was set up in the town's hotel. It was open to those who had lived within the corporation boundary. Six hundred of Newtownards' population of 3,000 were given free soup, and a small charge was made for bread. The kitchen cost £10 per week, with one third of the budget met by Robert Edward Ward, the local landowner. However, the operation was unable to feed all that needed help. No more money was to be had. In the rural districts surrounding Bangor, Lord Dufferin of Clandeboye and Robert Perceval Maxwell of Finnebrogue and Groomsport made arrangements to buy soup from the Bangor soup kitchen and to distribute it to the paupers on their estates.

How effective the private soup kitchens and the workhouses were in relieving poverty was pointed out in the *Banner of Ulster*. A reporter made many visits to houses in the region, and he was able to obtain first-hand information on the suffering. His reports put in no doubt the very urgent situation experienced in February 1847. The most serious cases were those where there was no work to be had, and the head of the house was unable to support his family. Families sold their possessions; and in some cases they ate nothing for several days. Some families chewed raw turnip or every few days they had small meals, bought with the proceeds of 'flowering'. This was work carried out by girls, or (in the case of Bangor) through work done by children at the cotton mills. In many cases the families were weak with hunger and on the point of starvation.

Half of the labourers in the townlands west of Crawfordsburn, Ballymullan, Ballygilbert and Ballygrost could not keep their families in food, nor sow the fields or meet their landlords' claims. Dysentery and cholera were rampant. Comber was spared the worst of the famine, but the state of the poor outside of the towns was not good. The *Banner of Ulster* reported that dysentery was still a problem. In the neighbourhood of Ballygowan there was an epidemic. Many labourers chose Scotland as a place of refuge, but the Scots were hard-pressed to support their own poor. Many of the small farmers had not a seed in the soil. Those that remained at Newtownards fell into the poverty trap. To them a meal a day was a luxury.

In Newtownards town the soup kitchen and the workhouse could not prevent suffering. Dysentery again proved to be the major problem arising from the want of the common necessities of life. A large proportion of the dead were in a wretched condition. Everywhere disease exacerbated the sufferings caused by famine. At Drumhirk, Ballyhinney, Loughriscouse and Ballyblack townlands there was hardly a labourer working in the fields. There was an absence of men ploughing in the spring. The annual ploughing match of Ards Farming Society, held near Greyabbey, was a failure. One observer said that labour was in a backward state. People were falling into apathy. In April 1847 it was noted that around Newtownards the great majority of the stockyards had no grain. The *Banner of Ulster* concluded that destitution was rife, especially in the south and west of Ireland. Maybe having so many poor at Newtownards affected negotiations between Andrews, on behalf of Lord Londonderry, and the Belfast & County Down Railway Company for land for a new railway line. Negotiations to develop land were under way by 18 January 1847 when the hunger was at its worst. Andrews was asking for as much as possible, and he admitted that he was asking a high price. The estimated rent for townland plots and for farms was beyond what could be afforded by the tenants. Negotiations dragged on for weeks, but by mid-May they were concluded. The railway company started work, employing labourers from the farms. If the negotiations had been completed earlier, the suffering of the poor might have been avoided.

74

At the peak of the famine a great argument arose about the attitude of the Marquess of Londonderry, as far as the suffering was concerned. An article in the *Londonderry Standard* of 8 January 1847 was entitled 'The Three Marquesses'. Its author was anonymous. The article alleged that, when it came to charity, the third marquess was not overgenerous – at least as far as Newtownards town was concerned. It said that Lord Londonderry had said that he would attend public meetings in Newtownards at the beginning of January, but at the last moment he had returned to London leaving his agent, Mr Andrews, to take his place. The sum total of Londonderry's subscription for relief was no more than £20. The Marchioness added £10 to her husband's gift. The article said that Andrews had written down a set of resolutions, tailored for the occasion. The author read them out, but some of those present left the meeting abruptly as a protest. The Marquess had made a great blunder when he supported the merchants and other well-to-do inhabitants of Newtownards. He was accused of having vain delusions and they said he behaved as though he believed that he was sent into the world merely to revel in the sweat and toil of others. He was without knowledge of others' beliefs.

Londonderry's contribution was compared to that of the Marquess of Downshire.

Andrews replied to the *Londonderry Standard* on Londonderry's behalf. He said that he had not chaired the relief meeting. He accused the *Londonderry Standard* of trying to disorganize the relationship between tenant and landlord. He pointed out that the Londonderrys had given £30 towards the soup kitchen as a first instalment. Lord Londonderry had raised the contribution to £50 and later gave another £50. The controversy took on a fresh twist when Andrews published another reply – this time in a rival newspaper, the conservative *Londonderry Sentinel*. He included a letter from Lord Londonderry himself, in which he said that he had not been approached about rent reduction in County Down. As far as he was concerned, there were adequate supplies at Newtownards, and the poor were provided for. He pointed out that Lady Londonderry had suggested setting up the soup kitchen, and that more money was available if required. He said that he was entirely willing to look after his tenants and his own town of Newtownards. He distributed poor relief to the paupers, but added that the poor should be independent. He said that he believed that he had never acted wrongly as a landlord or as a Christian. Lady Londonderry signed her own name: Vane Londonderry.

The editor of the *Londonderry Standard* said that Lord Londonderry had received applications for rent reduction and a few months later he published a statement saying he had decided not to make a rent reduction despite the onset of the potato famine. The editor compounded Lord Londonderry's donations with those of three or four insignificant muslin manufacturers. They, however, were anxious about the state of their starving tenants. The editor mocked Lord Londonderry's claim to have never acted wrongly as a Christian. He said Londonderry was in a most enviable state of inward blessedness, for some of the Apostles themselves could scarcely have made a more devout declaration.

Andrews saw the controversy in the widest terms: the position was that, as the landlord class stated, there was warfare against property and possessions. The *Londonderry Standard* reported that the policy should be to bring the people into the centre of the controversy. It said that the landlords were not at first open to liberal ideas. The editor, Dr James McKnight, was formerly the editor of the *Belfast Newsletter* and the Presbyterian newspaper, the *Banner of Ulster*. The editor was well known as a radical champion of tenants' rights. He might have been attempting to stir up discontent on the County Down estates.

In Londonderry's defence it must be said that he had increased his contribution to the Poor Law rates. This supported the workhouse to the large sum of £500 per year. Links were set up between two of his estates and his colliers in Durham, and this provided some work for the unemployed. Many people were also employed on drainage schemes. Lord Londonderry could be insensitive, but in 1848 the Londonderrys made extensive additions to their manor at Mount Stewart at a cost of £15,000. This created temporary work. It was seen by some as an attempt at relief, but to others it appeared to be the exploitation of the poor – if they have not got bread, give them cake. The grand opening took place in late November of that year. The *Downpatrick Recorder* said that Mount Stewart, with its spacious apartments, was open throughout the year to the gentry. They began to arrive after nine o'clock. The band of the 13th Regiment was in attendance, and at about ten o'clock dancing commenced, which lasted until one o'clock. There was a lavish new dining hall prepared for the reception of one hundred guests, who provided a display of fashion and beauty seldom seen in County Down. The Londonderrys bent over backwards to entertain their guests. After supper, festivities continued into the early hours of the morning.

The most important consideration was that Lord Londonderry did not have access to his entire fortune, but he had an annual income of £200 per annum. About £175 was Lady Londonderry's. His fortune was tied up in a trust which he could not touch. He was obliged to make his

Irish estates self-sufficient. The ground rental for his County Down estates was £23,000 with a further £2,000 from counties Londonderry and Donegal. When salaries, subscriptions, arrears and interest payments were deducted, he ended up with a deficit of £2,000 per annum. The Belfast Banking Company requested him to pay his debts in June 1847 or they would make Andrews liable for them.

A rift developed between some of the Newtownards guardians about relief provision. This went right to the heart of the debate surrounding famine relief.

At the peak of the crisis some landlords were not confident that they could carry through their objectives with regard to the poor in the union. When outdoor relief was provided, some decided to take advantage of the new legislation – the Temporary Relief Act, or the Soup Kitchen Act – of 17 February 1847. This enabled guardians, from February to September, to give or sell soup from the soup kitchens without the paupers having to come into the workhouses. New legislation came into force to establish permanent outdoor relief after September 1847. Costs were paid from the rates. Even before the Act could be passed, the Newtownards guardians sent a letter to the Relief Commissioners in Dublin informing them that the number of inmates was 832. They warned that if the workhouse took on any more inmates, malignant disease would break out. To avoid such a catastrophe, the measures that would help the poor should be passed through Parliament without any delay.

On 3 March 1847 the board voted by nineteen votes to eleven that a petition should be submitted to the House of Commons proposing extensive outdoor relief. It was hoped that this would be as extensive as the Irish Poor Law Act, and that it would help the poor, the destitute, and those disabled by age, mental or physical infirmity, sickness or accident. They should have the right to medical relief outside the workhouses. Everyone might suffer as a result of the workhouses being full.

New legislation was to be passed that would give them the right to change their status from beggars and that the government should provide subsidies. Now it was made difficult for mothers of illegitimate children to get into the workhouse, though they accepted that it would be in order that they should act as guardians for orphaned and deserted children or to otherwise provide relief. The government agreed to provide funds for the poor to emigrate to the British colonies. The board of guardians at Newtownards were experiencing many problems and they felt that they could not cope. Andrews was in the minority when the guardians voted on the petition. He said that he greatly dreaded the creation of a legal right to outdoor relief. It would greatly increase the number of claimants, and it might in the end generate all the evils of the old English Poor Laws.

The crisis was deepening and, in March, Andrews and the committee organized an additional round of subscriptions to the soup kitchen. Lord Londonderry headed the new list, donating another £50. Throughout the spring and early summer the hospital was starting to fill up to capacity, and the poor were suffering from dysentery. It was arranged that the medical officer be given an assistant. The medical officer reported that a number of paupers had died. The gravedigger was busy, and he was criticized for not burying the dead at least two feet below the ground. The guardians had to seek new ground for an additional cemetery. Some houses were rented near the workhouse as additional accommodation for the fever hospital.

Andrews liked this arrangement whereby the Temporary Relief Act, or Soup Kitchen Act, was invoked. He thanked God that the guardians' views did not affect his locality. He hoped that Newtownards would not engage in outdoor relief, despite the fact that a majority of the guardians had earlier suggested such legislation. Andrews was successful: by 14 May 1847 he was able to report, with pride, to Lord Londonderry, that matters were continuing as before to high standards. However, there was of course universal dependence upon relief afforded by the Temporary Relief Act. The voluntary soup kitchens (in Comber and Newtownards) were able to relieve distress which the workhouse could not deal with. The poor were to be evicted.

The crisis, despite the optimism, had not passed. In May, Andrews said that the workhouse contained 750 persons, with nearly 100 in the fever hospital. Heavy rates were on the point of being levied again. Although suffering was less than elsewhere there was not much hope for the future. The widespread importation of grain in the late spring and early summer relieved the situation: Food prices dropped. The soup kitchen was closed down in August 1847, after it had been in operation for only about six months. This meant that the only provision for the poor was now the workhouse. Outdoor relief had been made legal. In August, Andrews told Lord Londonderry that the potato crop seemed to be in a very precarious position. The disease was again spreading. There was little hope of small farmers holding their ground.

There was a test to enter the workhouse, and this was Andrews's method of coping with the suffering. He did not like outdoor relief and he was reluctant to allow its application. This brought him and his supporters into direct conflict with other guardians – and the law. The Poor Law Amendment Act, passed in July 1847, sought to deal with poverty wherever it occurred. The boards of guardians were now compelled to provide outdoor relief for those disabled by age or by temporary circumstances – for example, sickness or accident. The guardians were ordered to appoint relieving officers to assess the poor. Controversy raged amongst the Newtownards guardians over principles and the costs of the new scheme. Many of the leading guardians resigned over the issue.

The first shots were fired on 21 July 1847 at a meeting held by Edward Senior, the Poor Law Commissioner for East Ulster. He wanted to supervise the introduction of the new legislation. A resolution was proposed that would implement the new legislation at their next meeting. An amendment was passed stating that it was considered unnecessary to make provision for outdoor relief at present. William Sharman Crawford, the chairman, said that he dissented from this amendment because it was illegal; and also because the accommodation in the workhouse had been extended by using galleries as sleeping rooms for adults and lesser rooms for infants. He said that the workhouse seemed incapable of looking after the poor. The following week, Crawford said that the sleeping apartments for adults in the workhouse were overcrowded and that there was a public-health hazard. The same situation existed where the infants and young children were kept.

On 18 August the boards of guardians received formal instruction from the Poor Law Commissioners to appoint relieving officers. On 1 September the battle lines had been drawn up. Andrews pushed through a series of recommendations. He said that it was necessary to rely upon the workhouse, and that outdoor relief was a curse and a promoter of great social evil. He was sure that he could expand his own workhouse to meet the requirements of the poor.

William Sharman Crawford resigned as chairman within a few weeks, and Guy Stone and Robert Nicholson resigned as vice-chairmen. Crawford said that there were too many deaths in the house and that this was the result of overcrowding; he also said that people held out too long before resorting to charity, so, by the time many were admitted to the workhouse, they were seriously undernourished. He said that the workhouse test was unjust, uncharitable and unchristian.

Nicholson calculated that a labourer's family of five could be fed and clothed at the basic level of nine shillings per week. The guardians purchased everything below the market rate. It was impossible for labourers to earn a decent wage, so the workhouse was the only option.

A labourer would still be paying one shilling per week for the rent of his hovel. The number of those suffering from destitution was much greater than the number who applied to enter the workhouse. The situation was made worse by those too sick and infirm to work. He proposed a law which treated poverty as a crime, and provided relief for the poor. Neither confinement or restraint should be used as punishment.

The majority of the board resigned and followed the policies suggested by Andrews, who said that giving out free food was not wise and should be confined to private charity. He was wary of giving anything but essentials. The dividing line between public and private charity was clearly defined. The state declared that no one should die as a result of want of work.

The voluntary arrangements made in Andrews's area of Comber were considered to be excellent. Reflecting the view of political economy, he believed that outdoor relief encouraged the paupers into a state of dependency. His brother had just returned from Roscommon, where no grain was being cultivated. Rents were years in arrears and the poor rate was four shillings in the pound. The Young Irelanders, O'Connell's party, and the Tenants' Rights party, exploited the position. He was confident that the very best feeling existed amongst the people. They suffered greatly, but they were intent upon making the best of their difficulties and were anxious to do what they could. Andrews admitted that the poor were undernourished and that there was serious overcrowding in the workhouse. He pointed out that the mortality in the workhouse was very great between August and November. Many were demoralized by insufficient food before they sought refuge in the workhouse.

Prices were high and there was a food shortage. People were generally undernourished before they entered the workhouse, and this was attributed to the hand of God. Andrews, referring to the soup kitchen, added that voluntary funds were being raised to assist it. Andrews pointed out the crowded nature of the workhouse. Additional sleeping galleries were built as well as a wooden house in the yard. The charity would build and build to protect themselves against the practice of outdoor relief. Outdoor relief was a major concern and this was mentioned in the *Banner of Ulster* in relation to the situation at the Newtownards' soup kitchen. This was only satisfactory in a temporary way. Was it right that those in distress, because of unusual conditions, should be made to wait until they were destitute, and then be forced to enter an overcrowded workhouse? Deaths in the workhouse were considered by some as excessive. By November 1848 the Newtownards guardians were receiving complaints from the parishes that the graveyards were full up with those that had died in the workhouse. They had to purchase an area of ground for the paupers.

Andrews viewed the famine as a means by which to civilize the country. This, according to J. S. Donnolly, was the common view amongst the elite. Andrews argued that the effects of the Corn Laws would create a free market in grain and that there would have to be increased efforts from Irish farmers to compete. No encouragement should be given to idlers. Permanent trade in corn would require the efforts of everyone, and no one should be encouraged to lean back upon the poor rate. He was confident that he could employ his own men and that he would be able to grant agents a place in the running of the workhouse. If there were no more potatoes, it was hoped that the poor could be fed by other means. It was hoped that the regeneration of Ireland would come about as a result of these stringent conditions.

The estates of small tenants were cleared. This was either voluntary or forced. Andrews desired that the paupers should think about emigration. In August 1847 he observed that there was little chance for small farmers in conditions that prevailed during the famine. He could not see them holding their ground. He feared that the consequences for many of the poor would be terrible and, therefore, that the difficulty of realizing rental during the famine would be greatly increased. He was concerned that the tenants would start selling their cattle to raise rents. This would affect the estates or kill the goose that laid the golden egg. Alas! he felt that by failing to threaten eviction he might be open to criticism for being too indulgent.

Andrews now resigned from the board of guardians and left others to direct the affairs of the union. In November he informed Lord Londonderry that the board of guardians had carried out its resolutions. A compromise was imposed with the commissioners on the terms suggested by Lord Clarendon. He had carried another resolution calling upon the Poor Law Commissioners to direct their architect to supply plans for the enlargement of the workhouse. Matters were not as urgent as during the previous years, but in all parts of the country the workhouses were overflowing.

The first resolution was to appoint relieving officers for the rate collection. The idea was to extend the workhouse to accommodate 300 paupers. It is likely that Andrews held sway at the workhouse, but he could not continue to flout the law. In January 1848 Andrews and his men had to submit to new legislation. The Poor Law Commissioners did not like the idea of building an extension to the workhouse and insisted upon outdoor relief. This brought about a bitter resolution, carried by fourteen votes to eight. The guardians said that at these times of great poverty there was a lack of resources to feed the poor, but it was important to keep up standards of cleanliness and necessary discipline. The board of guardians at Newtownards was divided about the introduction of Poor Law relief. The voting pattern pointed to a geographical division in the union. For example, the guardians at Bangor were in favour of outdoor relief. At one stage they wished to have Poor Law relief in the electoral division of Bangor alone. The boards of guardians were left to settle amongst themselves their differences of opinion on the constitution of the Poor Law guardians. One explanation relates the decision to the great suffering in the area, but this does not shed much light upon a number of key issues. Nearly all ex officio guardians were in favour of outdoor relief, and most of these were landlords. Robert Gordon of Florida Manor was the only ex officio officer with Andrews to oppose outdoor relief. He declined to take over as chairman of the board. He said that most of the landlords were in favour of outdoor relief, but he wished to raise his voice in protest against moves to establish outdoor relief with its attendant evils. He could not request any compromise made between the boards of guardians and landed proprietors. He apologized for not taking up the office. It was clear that most of the landlords favoured outdoor relief, even though they were genuinely concerned about the state of their tenants. Crawford's and Nicholson's letters of resignation reflected these views. Or were they concerned with growing lawlessness or the cost of supporting the paupers? If outdoor relief was cheaper, the majority of the elected guardians would have followed them. Outdoor relief, in fact, was much more expensive, for it entailed the employment of relieving officers. Could it have been that those in favour of outdoor relief were the only ones that were able to be generous? There were other questions. Why did Andrews and Gordon, who were representatives of landed interests, differ from other landowners? Had they wider political interests? In the next few years the Londonderrys' interests and Robert Gordon's were criticized by the tenants' rights organization, in which William Sharman Crawford and Guy Stone took leading parts.

The crisis was over by the spring of 1848. In the quarter from April to July 1847, the population of the Newtownards workhouse peaked at 426; by July 1848 it had fallen to ninety-nine. The policy of outdoor relief perhaps explains the reduction in numbers. The Newtownards guardians were released of their burden of having to deal with a local crisis. . In 1848 their attention shifted to having to pay for the great calamity still being enacted beyond their union. They tried to avoid paying a tax that had been introduced to enable the more solvent unions to fund the poorest of the poor.

So far attention has been drawn to events in only part of County Down. This was considered to be the wealthiest part of the country, but even in Newtownards there was intense suffering.

If we look at another prosperous area, a similar situation can be found. Banbridge, said to be one of the busiest linen-manufacturing towns in Ireland and the flourishing centre of well-cultivated and fertile districts, also experienced considerable distress. According to Lewis's topographical dictionary (1837) there was great distress. Numbers in the workhouse rose from 259, to 1,107 in February 1847. High levels were recorded for the next few years, but they were at their peak in the first week of 1848. The master of the workhouse was unable to admit all those that sought admission, and some people refused to be turned away. These folk were said to be in a most destitute state, exhibiting symptoms of starvation. Some died. The master was ordered by the guardians to call in the constabulary to disperse the poor, but they were provided with some food so that they could make the journey home. Banbridge Choral Society gave a dress concert in the Town Hall in order to raise some money for a relief committee. A committee also operated at Loughbrickland. But not everyone was so charitable: John Joseph Whyte evicted a large number of tenants who were unable to pay their rents, as he wanted to make some changes in the landed property of the country to suit the altered circumstances of the times. J. P. Kelly encouraged remaining tenants to tend to their pastures and crops. To bring this about farms were enlarged. Such policies were the talk of all of Ulster and all of Ireland. Between 1841 and 1845 the population of the Banbridge Union fell from 87,000 to 75,000.

The Napoleonic Wars had pushed agricultural prices high for farmers in the barony, and decay had already set in when the potato blight hit the region. Hugh Wallace, the seneshal of Downpatrick, at the request of the parish priest, covered a meeting of the town's inhabitants at which it was decided to provide free meal and soup. Four hundred families took advantage of this. Soup kitchens were set up in every parish in the barony. At Killyleagh between thirty and fifty women gave meals to the poor every day. At Killough soup was provided from the end of 1846. Smallpox broke out in Downpatrick in 1847, and over 200 patients were admitted to the fever hospital and the workhouse. By August 1849 cholera broke out in the town and half of the fifty patients who were treated died.

It was in South Down that the suffering was greatest. Captain Brereton, the Board of Works inspecting officer, said that Rathfriland was the most badly affected area. At Castlewellan, women and children were described as weak and feeble by October 1846. Hunger was stalking the streets. The season was wet, and turf could not be obtained. Coals were out of the question. The continued cry amongst small farmers was that they did not know what to do. Rents were now called for and there was no money to meet the demands. Peasants were turned out of their holdings. The travails of the cottiers and day labourers were sad in the extreme. Their accustomed food had perished and no substitute was forthcoming. Their wages would have had to be trebled to be of any effect. They were offered eight or ten pence per day.

The landlords of South Down did not turn up at the relief meeting held at Castlewellan. They were criticized for wanting to head for England with their peasants' money in their pockets, leaving them to seek tender mercies from agents, whose pay depended upon the amount wrung from the unfortunate clans committed to their care. All the meeting could do was to ask the Lord Lieutenant to order an extraordinary presentment session for the barony to levy a new rate to provide urgent relief. On 30 December the Marquess of Downshire circulated a handbill objecting to such sessions. Once the session did meet, a few days later, some 6,000 people in rags met outside the courthouse at Castlewellan to ensure that a rate would be struck. With great difficulty Captain Brereton persuaded men of property to vote. He said that among the landed proprietors there was a great desire to relieve the poverty of the people.

The poor of his union were forced to wait by their social superior until they had become weak, almost to starvation point, although the worst months had seen the operation of privately financed soup kitchens. It was insisted that they came into the overcrowded workhouse, even though there was a risk of death through fever. Policies were shaped by previous ideas of political economy, and were carried out by the wealthier tenant farmers led by Lord Londonderry's agent, John Andrews. The bigger landlords tried without success to have outdoor relief administered. Andrews hoped that the smaller farmers would emigrate so that agriculture would become modernized to cope with the new situation after the repeal of the Corn Laws. This idea may have backfired, for it was not necessary for the poor to emigrate. The *Downpatrick Recorder* pointed out that much wealth, in the form of people, was being sent to the United States. The Down peasantry were on the move west. Two thousand poor left their districts of Newtownards,

Lecale and other parts of the country for emigration to America, but they did not leave Ulster with empty purses. In one emigrant ship alone, which sailed from Belfast, more than a fourth of the passengers were from County Down.

These policies reduced the area population. It is not possible to ascertain the number that died in the Newtownards Union during the potato famine, but many of those weakened, because of high food prices, died of typhus and dysentery. The population of the Newtownards Union in 1837 was about 53,837; in 1841 it had risen to 60,285. One might expect the population to have increased to about 63,000 by the time of the 1851 census. Between 1840 and 1851 the population of the parish of Newtownards had fallen by fourteen per cent. It eventually fell by over twenty per cent.

The troubles damaged landlord–tenant relationships. There was a direct relationship between the famine and the tenants' rights organization. At Newtownards, hostility was directed towards Lord Londonderry at a meeting held in the town, but Andrews wrote seeking to console him. He said that he was sorry that His Lordship had been put out, but he said that nothing more should be expected from such people. Others had contradicted Andrews's assessment. The *Newtownards Chronicle* in 1893 referred to the dangers of rioting and breakdown in law and order. At the time of the famine, one David McKean was a highly respected agent in the town for Messrs Brown. Muslin was required by Glasgow merchants, and this gave employment to the poor. David McKean eventually became an assistant to Lord Londonderry's agents from 1862 to 1887. He was an elder of Newtownards 2nd Presbyterian Church. Forty-five years later he still influenced the running of the town. Again there was unemployment, despite his efforts to subsidize the poor. Threats of bread riots were voiced.

A general election was held in 1857. The voting was concerned with the position of tenants' rights, and the terrible state of the peasantry during the famine. As an act of defiance, they refused to vote for Lord Londonderry's candidate. Instead William Sharman Crawford was victorious. Londonderry now evicted seventy tenants who were in arrears of rent and had voted against his wishes. However, he made many grants to charities in the area. The Great Hunger marked the beginning and the end of the defiance. It is difficult to ascertain how the building of the Londonderry Monument in 1854 came about. Perhaps Lord Londonderry was generous to the population during the 1850s, but a study of the subscriptions does not support such a conclusion. Relations were strained in the town, according to other evidence. 1848 was a time of revolutions all over Europe, and in Ireland, the Young Irelanders wanted a repeal of the Act of Union. The government, in retaliation, sought Catholic alliances throughout the island. In April 1848 Andrews suggested that Lord Londonderry should prepare himself for the worst, in view of conditions in the parishes of Newtownards and Comber. The principal inhabitants were invited to make suggestions without the risk of holding a public meeting. Towards the end of April 1848 a private meeting of the most influential inhabitants of Newtownards was held with this in mind. The Newtownards nationalists, led by John McKittrick (a guardian and a local draper) and the parish priest, had already made a submission declaring that Newtownards sought repeal of the Act of Union. The meeting said that a petition should be sent; but, as Andrews said to Lord Londonderry, he desired him to request a public meeting which they feared might be difficult to assemble, for such meetings were often held in the union.

There were other consequences of a religious nature. According to the *Newtownards Independent*, commenting twenty-five years later, the weavers after the famine were not in the same condition as they were before it. Saturday-night squabbling had ceased. Business had fled from the public houses. Prayer meetings were established at places where cock fighting, dog fights and animal hunting were prohibited on Sunday. Seriousness everywhere prevailed. Number of Bibles, hymn books and Psalm books were fished from all sorts of places.

Chapter 6

The Great Hunger in County Fermanagh

Between the years 1841 and 1851 the population of Fermanagh dropped from 156,481 to 116,047 according to the census. This represented a decline of twenty-five per cent. Of the eight baronies in County Fermanagh, that of Magheraboy lost thirty-one per cent of its population. Magheraboy runs from Enniskillen towards the west and excludes the villages of Derrygonnelly and Garrison. The latter was worst affected and lost thirty-one per cent of its population. In the baronies of Clanawley and Clankelly twenty-eight per cent of the population was lost.

The barony of Lurg in the west of the county, which includes the villages of Belleek, Irvinestown, Kesh and Edendery, lost twenty-seven per cent of its population. Those least affected were the baronies of Magherastephana, Knockninny and Tirkennedy, where the population declined by twenty-two per cent and eleven per cent respectively. Tirkennedy, which suffered least decline, included Enniskillen (the county town), and Tempo. The small decline here reflected migration from other parts of the county into Enniskillen as well as the additional population of the workhouse. Part of this migration into Enniskillen was by the tenants of Lord Belmore from County Cavan. They came in expectation of whatever relief the landlord might have to offer.

In some townlands the percentage population was even greater than this but there is no way of telling the exact numbers of farmers affected or the movements of people to the region. In the Belleek region, and in the village of Belleek the numbers grew during the famine, pointing to movements from townlands nearby. Other townlands grew on account of people moving into them as the exodus was set in motion. Today the impact of the famine in County Fermanagh may be measured by the fact that Fermanagh has only one third of the population that it had in 1841.

It is said that the potato famine first made its appearance in Ulster in County Fermanagh. The famine only reached Fermanagh slowly, and this was one of the four centres that did not have a relief committee in 1845 when the first outbreaks of the disease occurred over a large part of Ireland. The workhouse had been partly built in County Fermanagh prior to 1845: at Irvinestown in the west, in the centre, and at Lisnaskea in the east help was forthcoming. The Enniskillen workhouse had been built in 1842, but it wasn't until the autumn of 1845 that it was in effective operation. At either end of the county, workhouses at Clones in County Monaghan and Ballyshannon in County Donegal served the extremities of County Fermanagh.

After the initial fear in the autumn of 1845 (which did not seriously affect Fermanagh) some of the relief that the blight had not taken root in the county was expressed. A guardian landstewart in the Coolebrook estate sent a letter, which was published in the local press in December 1845. He said that the tenantry in the Coolebrook property were nearly free from the potato famine. A considerable number of the potatoes had, however, been in pits for the past six weeks. After a regular and minute examination of them up to date he had discovered some diseased potatoes. He went on to say that he had made very narrow pits covered with sods. Sir Arthur Brook returned from England to visit most of the tenants and he was careful to emphasize the necessity of securing sufficient seed for the coming spring. He recommended frequent rewards for any reports that might indicate decay. He was happy that the neighbourhood around Brookeborough was nearly as fortunate as some other places in the county. In November 1845 the *Enniskillen Chronicle and Erne Packet* criticized farmers who exploited the poor by selling them bad potatoes. The paper called attention to the state of the potato markets. Great caution needed to be exercised to prevent the spread of diseased potatoes, but farmers wanted to get rid of decayed potatoes. The evil this would inflict upon the poor needed to be guarded against in the town. A sad instance was reported of a poor man who gave a shilling for potatoes, but discovered that the potatoes were uneatable. A female purchased two stone of potatoes, but when she boiled them she found to her grief that they were diseased. Only a few were eatable. It behoved those in authority to devote some energy, for humanity's sake, to put an end to this practice.

In 1845, following the alarm over the potato crop in the autumn and winter, as reported by newspapers in other parts of Ireland, County Fermanagh, with trepidation, awaited the results of the harvest in the following year. The local newspaper carried very few stories about the famine. Accounts concerned conditions in the workhouses, the reduction of rents by landlords, and instances of deaths and starvation in the towns and villages. There were also outrages committed when starving people broke into the meal stores, or killed animals in the fields at night. The first serious effects of the potato famine started to be felt at the beginning of the autumn of 1846, mainly in the workhouses, where the diet consisted entirely of potatoes. The Enniskillen workhouse continued to use potatoes, despite inflation, until July 1846, when oatmeal was substituted for the children's diet. A month later the adults were denied the potato diet; they were given seven ounces of oatmeal instead of the usual ration of potatoes. At a meeting in September 1846, the guardians were sent a letter from the Poor Law Commissioners concerning the general failure of the potato crop. They ordered that an adult male or female should be supplied with seven ounces of oatmeal and one pint of buttermilk for breakfast, and seven ounces of oatmeal and one pint of buttermilk for dinner. Boys and girls aged nine to eleven were supplied with three ounces of oatmeal and three noggins of buttermilk for breakfast.

In Lowtherstown, potatoes remained available until 1846. In January the guardians had been warned that the Poor Law Commissioners were giving the inmates three meals per day. By the end of 1846, a meeting was held to try to ascertain the extent of the blight and to offer advice on the situation. The November edition of the *Enniskillen Chronicle and Erne Packet* carried the story of the meeting. The headline was 'Potato Disease – Public Meeting in Enniskillen'. The meeting was held in the courthouse at twelve o'clock. It was convened by the Earl of Erne, lieutenant of the county, for the purposes of considering the state of the potato crop in County Fermanagh. The Earl and his committee sat in the Grand Jury Room to receive information from farmers and gentlemen before the start of the meeting.

Afterwards, the Earl read a document, drawn up by the committee, containing advice and presenting information on the subject of the failed crop of potatoes: first, on the best method to preserve good potatoes; secondly, on the best method to arrest the progress of the disease in potatoes already affected; and thirdly, on the turning of diseased potatoes into wholesome food. Cake-bread, made from the starch of tainted potatoes, was handed out.

Dr Halpin of Cavan was introduced to the meeting as a man who had studied the famine in detail. He proposed a ventilated pit to store potatoes. He was against the advice put forward at the time, which included digging potatoes in wet weather rather than in dry weather. The possibility was discussed of drying the crop over fires in basins full of hot water. During the autumn of 1846 it became evident that the potato crop was again failing on a grand scale. A meeting of tenants, landlords and landholders held in Lisbellaw in August 1846 said that potatoes were almost extinct and starvation was threatening. A meeting of 2,500 people in Brookeborough begged for relief. Crowds of people at Derrygonnelly asked to be employed. There was a run on the workhouses, which were mostly unprepared, but which were expected to provide relief. Large numbers of poor people put pressure on the workhouses, creating problems of hygiene, and risking the spread of disease. Conditions worsened and papers carried critical reports. When relief work began, the *Erne Packet* condemned the poor conditions. Relief was provided by forcing the destitute to labour on various works. The report also made the point that Sir Robert Peel had at least made an effort to handle the problem. The headline was 'Death from Starvation'.

On the morning of 16 December 1846 a man named James Roulston of Rohall in the region of Lowtherstown was discovered dead in a field near his own house. On the previous morning he had left his family of six and he had gone to repair the works at Drumskool, where he was employed at ten pence per day. He had worked all day in bad weather and he wanted food. On his return that night through fields covered in snow, he gave in to exhaustion. The only sustenance he had was a few turnips and their stalks.

An inquest was held on the body of James Roulston at Enniskillen the next day, and the verdict was that he had died from fatigue and not from insufficient nourishment. The newspaper went on to exclaim, 'Good God, what a state matters have come to!' There were people dying because of inaction. It was declared that the situation was bad, but under Russell's administration one could speculate that things could be on the turn. It was thought that Sir Robert Peel was the right man to cope with the situation, and there should be no delay in providing solutions. The country was being decimated at present. The poor workers did not have the price of a pound of meal, and the workhouses were overflowing. In Irvinestown the workhouse was forced to lease many buildings in the town to accommodate the overflow of those who wanted shelter, some of whom had been evicted from their homes.

Between September 1846 and May 1847 there were reports in the *Enniskillen Chronicle and Erne Packet* that fever and famine were causing havoc amongst the population. At Enniskillen, hungry children were unable to buy soup from the soup kitchen. At Currin a woman lay dead for three days before burial. At length she was carried like a dead hog and incompletely buried by two weak women. She lay partly exposed until the sexton buried her. In Garvery Wood hundreds of corpses were buried. They were the victims of cholera, and their relations were too weak to carry them to the graveyard. At Kinawley a young girl died, and her friends, fearing the fever, put her on a bier at once and set out for the graveyard.

By the end of 1846 potatoes were selling at one shilling per stone in Enniskillen. Riots broke out in the market as speculators tried to buy up supplies and take them out of the area. Indian meal sold at ten pence per stone, and rice at twopence per pound. Preference was given to the cleaner potatoes. People detested these kinds of food. Added to their misery was a lack of information on how to cook them. Indian meal had to be steeped overnight in water to make it eatable, and failure to do so added additional illnesses to the burden of those dying of starvation. By 1847 the government acknowledged the scale of the tragedy. The Poor Law system had the main responsibility for organizing relief. Soup kitchens were established, but already some folk, such as the county surveyor, had been organizing this form of relief at Enniskillen and Lisbellaw. At first the poor had to pay for their portion, but after a while this was abandoned. By the summer of 1847 there were 2,000 people being fed by the Enniskillen soup kitchen, while at Maguiresbridge 2,700 were catered for.

Doctors, clergy, members of the boards of guardians and workhouse staff also died. Nowhere was there safety. At Enniskillen, Dr Condon and Dr Frith died of fever, as also did one of the guardians. The workhouse smelled, and this drove the board of guardians to hold their meetings in the Town Hall. Up to twenty people died in the Enniskillen workhouse every day. Temporary fever hospitals sprang up in the villages around Enniskillen. In mid-December 1847 there were 879 people in the Enniskillen workhouse, which had been built to hold 1,000. By mid-January the number of occupants was 1,137. By May of the following year this had risen to 1,433.

At their January meeting, the Enniskillen guardians directed the authorities to admit no further paupers, except in cases of chronic destitution. The workhouse was now crowded to excess. The Enniskillen workhouse also exceeded its capacity of 1,000, and the same was now the case at Lisnaskea and Lowtherstown. In January 1846 the Lowtherstown workhouse had fifty-one poor; a year later, in January 1847, it exceeded its limit with 453 paupers. One hundred and sixty more inmates were added to the Enniskillen workhouse, probably because they were severely destitute, as the guardians had ruled. By 5 February the number of new inmates had been reduced to five, although the problem of overcrowding still mounted. The pressure put on the authorities was, from late 1846, being increasingly felt by the three workhouses which served the county. This is shown by the capacities for each workhouse – Enniskillen, 1,000; Lisnaskea, 500; and Lowtherstown, 400.

The two workhouses at Lowtherstown and Lisnaskea were filled to capacity from December 1846. Enniskillen also exceeded its capacity for the following months. By the end of 1847 Enniskillen continued to be filled to capacity, and the two smaller workhouses were in an unworkable state. By the end of the following year, 1848, the pressure had eased somewhat in the Lowtherstown workhouse, but it was still operating at 150 per cent of its capacity. Lisnaskea had 321 more inmates than it was designed for and Enniskillen exceeded its limit by 557. As early as April 1847, the conditions inside the Enniskillen workhouse were of great concern to Dr Nixon, the medical officer, who reported to the guardians that the sewers had overflowed and flooded the laundry room, and that this was causing disease. Refuse was dumped beside the house, and warm weather would make the situation extremely dangerous. The drying room had been converted into a nursery. There was no means of drying the straw used by those who had slept on the floor. There was no ventilation in the house and the rooms were never cleaned. There were no facilities for inmates to wash themselves. Meals were inadequate. A new fever hospital was required as one hundred patients lay on thirty beds in Halls Lane. Water supplies were also inadequate. In the workhouse there were only sixty beds. The remainder of the inmates slept on the floor. There were few items of furniture. There were only two nurses to 312 patients.

The problem was chronic. The Enniskillen guardians' position was exacerbated by continual overcrowding. By May 1847 they were in debt to the tune of £5,000. This brought them into contact with the Poor Law Commissioners. When they applied to the government for a loan of between £3,000 and £4,000 they were given a grant of £100 and told to collect an added rate if necessary. The guardians did not like the idea and said that the imposition of an additional rate on the ratepayers would bring ruin. The guardians exclaimed that no system could be more dishonest in principle or more mischievous. Far from resolving the situation, the conflicts between the Enniskillen guardians and the Poor Law Commissioners continued until the Enniskillen board of guardians was dissolved at the end of 1847.

Two of the three County Fermanagh workhouses were among the four boards of guardians in Ulster that were dissolved when responsibility for relief passed to them. The Lowtherstown Union also approached the Poor Law Commissioners to the extent that it was dissolved. As was the case in Enniskillen, the Lowtherstown guardians felt that it was wrong to ask the local ratepayers to shoulder the entire burden. As was the case in many other unions, the amount raised from local rates was insufficient to meet the demands being made. When the Poor Law became the only means of relief, the additional burden proved too much even though the burden of the poor rates was not particularly high in the Lowtherstown Union.

The Lowtherstown guardians did not take their punishment lying down. Vice-guardians were appointed in their place. They tried to bring in a new rate, but this was resisted, and occasionally violence was threatened against them. The original guardians were eventually restored in March 1849. They were the first board of guardians to be dismissed, and also the first to be reinstated. They started again to run the union, and they heaped abuse on the vice-guardians who had acted in their stead. They found the union as a whole much demoralized. The poor classes were told that, instead of looking for employment, they should place faith in God, and run their lives in accordance with a code. The pauper would now have to live by Act of Parliament alone.

The Lowtherstown (or Irvinestown) workhouse had been opened on 15 October 1845 after words had been exchanged between the local landlord and the board of guardians who served most of West Fermanagh. An investigation was held into the setting up of the workhouse. The report listed that (1) The commissioners fixed a site, and gave an exorbitant price for it before the board was formed. (2) The commissioners allowed the union to give £150 for tenants' rights. The total price was £647 19s. (3) A sum of £878 was given to the contract. (4) A building with equal accommodation might have been built for less money.

Mr Justice Pennethorn, who investigated the allegations of gross overpayment for the site of the workhouse, stated that it appeared that the only point in which he was employed was to cover expenses to the tune of £697 19s., and this was an exorbitant price for the site. Whether Mr Darcy was paid £50 or £500 was of no importance to the commissioners. They had only to give the full value for the land, without reference to money. It appears that no one was appointed to possess the site. The assistant commissioner was incompetent, and so was the assistant architect, and they found it difficult to express a view on the subject. Mr Darcy named his price. This was reported to the commissioners and they forthwith, by a letter of 28 January, virtually agreed to the terms. Before the letter of 2 March, and before they realized it, a title could be made; and, before the question of expense could be settled, they began to build the workhouse. They placed themselves at Darcy's mercy and were thus in a position to pay his price. Prices paid for the workhouse sites were as follows: Lowtherstown, £139 1s.; Omagh, £125 6s.; Enniskillen, £153; Clones, £57 1s. 3d.; Lisnaskea £51 16s. 8d.

After the opening of the workhouse, complaints continued to flow in of mismanagement, until by 1847 the commissioners appointed vice-commissioners. During the tenure the building was finished and the sewage system went into use. The paupers' graveyard was prevented from sending its discharge into the workhouse yard. In the report of Denis Phelon, which led to the appointment of the vice-commissioners, the condition of the workhouse was described as the worst in the north of Ireland.

The Enniskillen workhouse was one of the few workhouses not to be dissolved. Controversy surrounded the deliberations of the Lisnaskea guardians, who had assembled to consider the government demand for an increase in the Rate-in-Aid in support of the administration of additional relief schemes in 1849. By now the failure of the crop had given rise to fever, disease and homelessness. People were becoming increasingly apprehensive. The minutes of the board's discussions, and their letter to the Poor Law Commissioners, show a collectively angry outburst. There was talk about the workhouse and the demands put upon it. This was indicative of adverse times. They said that it was with indignation that they had to impose the Poor Law on the inhabitants of Ulster, for the support of the lazy, vicious and indolent population of the south and west of Ireland. It was said that they neither feared God or honoured the Queen, nor had they respect for those who had lost land.

They were approached about the introduction of the Poor Law into County Fermanagh, and, when it became the law of the land, the guardians of the union used all their endeavours to impose the law efficiently and with good effect. They gave shelter to the homeless and food to those who could not work.

The ratepayers of the union, with the principle of honesty foremost, helped the inhabitants of the north of Ireland. This helped them over a period of distress. With the greatest industry they paid their rates. They said that in other parts the military and the magistrates collected the poor rate. Resistance to the Poor Law was rendered inappropriate. The guardians firmly believed that they reflected the views of all ratepayers in the union as well as those in the province of Ulster generally.

Of the first 440 entries to the workhouse, 221 were Roman Catholic and 218 were Protestant. Later, one third of the workhouse entries were Protestant.

There were more young people in the workhouse than old people, and there were few in the age range twenty-to-forty. The workhouse was largely filled with children and old people. The workhouse was sixty per cent female and forty per cent male. About seventy per cent of the total entries had addresses in the two electoral divisions closest to Irvinestown itself. At first people came and went to the workhouse quite freely. One couple were recorded as having made several short visits. There were complaints of people falling down in the village and of having been fitted out in new clothing. Farm boys and girls entered in November, after being told to do so by their employers, who wished to have them fed by the workhouse in the least productive part of the year. During 1847 just under eighty per cent of those entering the workhouse in Irvinestown were under fifteen years of age.

The administration of the Enniskillen workhouse was equally bogged down in controversy. Perhaps the most flagrant innovation was the introduction of a new type of coffin that did not require much wood. A slip coffin was constructed which had a mechanical spring and a false bottom. This reduced the cost of buying wood for coffins. The *Impartial Reporter* said that many in the town did not like burying their dead without coffins. The motion, however, was not voted upon and wood for chamber burials was purchased.

In January 1847 the pressure on the workhouse increased, and this was acknowledged by the Enniskillen guardians. They directed the master of the workhouse to admit no further paupers except in cases of great destitution, for the workhouse was now overcrowded. On 4 May, 351 men, women and children were admitted to Enniskillen workhouse at the same time. They had waited on the guardians of the workhouse all day. During the guardians' meeting they had made their way into the workhouse, much to the chagrin of the guardians. The *Impartial Reporter* said that children appeared to be dying from lack of food. Older people were propped up by relations, who were also dependent upon the support of the workhouse. The general appearance of these people was sickly and filthy. An attempt was made to enter their names, and some feared that they might be excluded. Another assessment was made and its findings were placed before the board. They rushed for the window and gasped for breath.

All were admitted as the twenty-six consecutive pages of the indoor admission register records. There were 163 adults admitted – sixty-seven males and ninety-six females – and 188 children under fifteen years of age. A study made by Joan Vincent recorded several significant factors in the aftermath of this episode. A hundred and eleven females died within three months. By the end of May, seventy-eight of the May admissions had perished. Another thirty-three deaths were recorded in June and ten in July. The great majority of these deaths were due to the contagion which was rife in the workhouse.

The fever hospital attached to the Enniskillen workhouse had been built to house 120. By the beginning of 1847 it was overcrowded. Death was a strong possibility for those paupers that fled to the workhouse during 1847. The workhouse was caring for up to 430 people, forty of whom were diagnosed as 'fever patients'.

The first entry in the admission register of the workhouse, preserved in the Public Record Office of Northern Ireland, provides a lot of information about the poor and their admission to the workhouse. This is illustrated in the record preserved about one pauper. He was described as a male, a beggar, aged seventy-five, and he was a Protestant. He had a wooden leg. He had no children and had been deserted by his wife. He was, however, clean and healthy but with no fixed address. His upkeep was regarded as a burden on the union. On 15 October he entered the workhouse, and he left eight days later. He re-entered on 5 November of the same year and left again after two days. He was admitted eight times to the workhouse.

Enniskillen's workhouse was, like that in Irvinestown, a delayed project. The cost of the site was disputed, which was also the case in Irvinestown. The Earl of Enniskillen was at the centre of the row after selling his site for a fixed price per acre. He was glad that it was an English acre rather than the larger Irish acre. This oversight by the Earl of Enniskillen was much to the annoyance of the other Poor Law guardians of Enniskillen, who, like other ratepayers, would have to pay the inflated price.

A similar row to the one at Irvinestown followed on this and other issues. It was some years before the workhouse was opened and the paupers admitted. Those who had to pay believed perhaps that they could obtain value for their money, but there were those that wanted to postpone the opening of the workhouse indefinitely. In the end, pressure from the Poor Law Commissioners forced the workhouse to open. On Thursday, 30 November 1845 the *Enniskillen Chronicle and Erne Packet* reported the opening of the workhouse. It said that the Enniskillen Union workhouse was at last about to be opened. It had remained idle for three years. The poor were now looked upon favourably in their plight. Country gentlemen and farmers had ignored or so far escaped taxation, but they assumed that their town had to bear a heavy burden to prevent absolute starvation and the spread of fever and contagion. The inhabitants of the Enniskillen workhouse were a jolly lot despite the hardships. They were paying their own rate; but of course there were still those that remained destitute. They continued to be victims of fever, and they hoped that the evil would end.

The Lisnaskea workhouse featured in the local newspaper of the period. It seemed to be reasonably well run and did not have an unenthusiastic beginning, unlike County Fermanagh's other two workhouses. A feature of the County Fermanagh workhouse population by 1848 was the unusual proportion of young people aged about fifteen that were reduced to pauperdom. In December 1846 there were 892 paupers in the Enniskillen workhouse, and 385 (forty-three per cent) were under fifteen years of age. This increased to forty-eight per cent; and then, by December 1848, to fifty-eight per cent. In Lowtherstown the proportion was forty-four per cent. Children with no means of support could also be found outside the workhouse. There was a danger they would become long-term inmates. This fear was shared by Edward Senior, the Poor Law inspector, who conveyed his alarm along with that of the guardians elsewhere in Ulster.

It came to light that there were some 107 female orphans under the Enniskillen guardians, and forty-four from Lisnaskea. The scheme took 4,000 other female orphans aged fifteen from workhouses throughout Ireland, and sent them to Australia between 1848 and 1850. As time passed, they made an important contribution to colonial society, and at the same time their emigration helped to reduce the numbers of orphans in Ireland's workhouses. There was a great preponderance of orphans in Ulster workhouses, where they amounted to fifty per cent of the total workhouse population. In other Irish provinces the figure was about forty per cent.

On 11 January 1849 the *Enniskillen Chronicle and Erne Packet* pointed out that the potato famine was no longer a problem, and this was also the position on some of the other estates. It was further stated that the blight was over. The potatoes were now sown in the soil, but there was the possibility of frost. Early planting was an effectual remedy for the potato rot. If the potatoes would avoid the frost there would be no shortage in that area. The influence, however, of what had been a fearful tragedy for County Fermanagh would last for generations. The story of the famine would be told in many Gaelic hovels and workhouses throughout County Fermanagh and the rest of Ireland.

Chapter 7

The Great Hunger in County Londonderry

The famine in County Londonderry does not seem to have been so severe as elsewhere in Ulster. There was no disease in the crop, none was known to farmers. However, the Royal Irish Constabulary sub-inspector, Nesbitt, wrote from Coleraine on 20 September 1845 and referred to reports that the potato crop of the year had totally failed. This was reflected in the summary report for the county submitted by the county inspector, George Fitzmaurice. He said that the disease did not exist to any great extent in County Londonderry, except in the district of Ballyrashane. Their confidence was misplaced. On 13 October, the medical officer to the Coleraine workhouse wrote to Babington, the chief secretary, in dismal terms. He said that reports of the disease were not exaggerated. Whole fields were unfit for habitation by man or beast. Such was the state of the crop that a great scarcity of food loomed. Typhus fever, or some other malignant disease, reared its head. Within less than a month, further police reports corroborated Babington's report. The report of 13 October said that the disease was spreading in his district to a great extent. By 4 November 1845 the Royal Irish Constabulary said that the famine in the district of Coleraine had started to hit the potatoes. One report estimated that the disease was in one third of the total potato crop. This caused great alarm in the poorer classes.

In the southern parts of County Londonderry the change from a healthy crop to tragedy had been observed earlier by the Reverend Samuel Montgomery, the rector of the parish of Ballynascreen. He later recalled that a memoir in his register in 1846, the following year, said that the entire crop had disappeared in the month of July. After August there were blackened and withered plants. The atmosphere in September was tainted with the smell of rotting potatoes. He added in his memoir that people should increase the fruit of the earth under heavenly benediction. The evidence of the newspapers, boards of guardians' minutes and parish registers indicate that the appearance of the potato blight was widely reported throughout County Londonderry. By mid-October, particularly in four out of the five unions which served the county – at Londonderry, Coleraine, Magherafelt and Ballymoney – conditions were getting worse. The accumulation of the disease was by mid-October occupying the attention of the guardians of the Londonderry and Coleraine workhouses. A letter had in fact been sympathetic about the death of the workhouse porter from typhus fever in September 1845, but this turned out to be an isolated occurrence. On 18 October the Londonderry guardians were of the opinion that the mayor should consult with the merchants and people of Londonderry to decide whether a public meeting should be held to discuss the possibility of a large quantity of food being available in the aftermath of the failure of the potato crop. Private and government agencies took steps to have the potatoes converted into starch. On the same day (18 October) the Coleraine guardians announced that in a week's time the board would consider what steps should be adopted to combat the disease that was likely to follow the failure of the potato crop.

The spread of the potato blight in County Londonderry was patchy – a feature characteristic of the first winter of the blight in the Ulster counties. This is evident in the Limavady Union, which seems to have been spared the terrors of the blight. The word from Newtown Limavady was that little corn and meal were abundant in the union. There were large markets of sound potatoes at Kilrea, Maghera and Magherafelt. The Lord Lieutenant of the county, Sir Robert Ferguson, wanted to adopt a more measured approach. He said that an absolute scarcity of food was dreaded, but it would be difficult for labourers to support their families. Employment would be brought about by work on the railways and by other works such as land reclamation on Lough Foyle. He trusted that the attention of the government should be directed on the relief required. He rounded off his views by saying that the landed proprietors should cooperate in their fight against the potato fever.

Christine Kinealy drew attention to the association of the landed classes with the work of local relief bodies, as a general measurement of the landlords' collective response to the increasing hunger, certainly as early as 1840, when the famine appeared to be more manageable. The response of landed proprietors in County Londonderry was evident in the formation of fourteen relief committees, which began to take shape throughout the county in the late winter and early spring of 1846, to cope with the challenge faced by the blight. The standard donation was £10, as offered by Marcus McCauseland of Fruithill to the Newtown Limavady Relief Committee. The *Coleraine Chronicle* was happy to learn that large amounts of meal that had been bought had now been resold to the poor of the estates at a reduced price. Between one and two hundred families were now receiving relief. The approach seems to have been that noted in the Claudy Relief Committee's submission. The landed proprietors had agreed to contribute in proportion to the value of their respective properties, as noted under the Poor Law Valuation.

Twenty-five relief committees were formed throughout County Londonderry, of which twenty received full grants from the government. It would match pound for pound amounts of money received locally. Londonderry Relief Committee raised £1,290; at Newtown Limavady £341 was raised; and the Coleraine committee raised £322. At first the generosity was not well received. At the inaugural meeting at Coleraine in April 1846, it was proposed that a subscription list should be opened on the spot and that each person should contribute a little. Several gentlemen voiced their dissent. The situation was becoming serious, and it was recorded that in the parish of Dunboe alone there were hundreds of people living on one meagre meal each per day. The landlords had great respect for the county town of Londonderry. However, here conditions were worse than in the south of Ireland. The second failure of the potato crop was enough to elicit a more thorough approach to the system of relief. Mr Knox now dealt with this second failure. In February 1847 he wrote to the treasurer of the Dunboe and Macosquin parishes requesting government aid for this greatly disorganized region.

The Aghadowey Relief Committee raised a total of £109. In April 1846 the deputations from the Ironmongers' estate, which had visited the village of Aghadowey, described the conditions as wretched. The potato blight reappeared: Aghadowey and other needy settlements throughout County Londonderry were in a perilous condition. It was pointed out that claims should be made out of public money, otherwise the destitute would go on until death from hunger prevailed. Successful efforts to avoid the famine were deserving of public assistance.

There was quite a good response from the general public to the position of the Gaels in regard to the famine. The potato blight was caught in its earliest stages. This can be attributed to the position of the tenants in those years immediately prior to the hunger. Londonderry was now also seriously affected. There had been a series of revivals in the Irish economy in the thirty years between the end of the Napoleonic Wars and the famine. The Ordnance Survey Memoirs and the Poor Law Inquiry each testified to the social consequences of the economic hardships provoked by the general fall in prices for agricultural produce. County Londonderry, with villages such as Aghadowey, had witnessed the serious decline in income previously derived from the cottage spinning industry. The coming of the mechanical spinning process in mills throughout Ulster meant poverty for many families. The Poor Law Commissioners of Inquiry had noted the increase in annual emigration and seasonal migration from the county in the years 1832–4. This is the strongest evidence available of the change in family fortunes arising out of the fall in incomes.

The extent of the 1830s crisis in the east of Ulster is shown in a series of petitions addressed to the agents at Draperstown. The company had repossessed its lands in 1817, so that more efficient systems could be adopted. This meant that the farmers would not overtly suffer from the hunger, and that the progress of subdivision would not continue.

The London Companies, which had taken possession of County Coleraine in the early years of the seventeenth century, were absentee landlords in a very fundamentalist sense. They had agents, however, and, if anything, they were improving the position of many resident landlords. A new broom was to sweep clean and was to be tempered with tolerance. This was evident in their submission to the companies' London headquarters. A large number of poor people had come to their attention during the 1830s, when the full extent of the reduction of incomes had started to become apparent. In their recommendation they encouraged the granting of relief for tenants where livelihoods were in peril and for those who, like William Jean Convey of Bracaghreilly, had fallen upon hard times. It was recorded that a petitioner's husband had died in August 1831, leaving a helpless family. After the death of her husband, the petitioner found herself unable even to pay the annual rent. There was a scarcity of money and there was no support for this helpless family.

The agents continued to grant relief to the many who opted for the workhouse, even before the full impact of the famine had become known in the winter of 1846/7. As early as November 1846 the agents drew attention to the probable distress that might occur if the agents did not do their jobs properly. Provisions were dear, and there was a want of employment for the poor. In many cases the tenants' circumstances were voiced and the company continued to pay for emigration. This was the situation in the spring of 1847. Widow Bradley of Ballygrooby said that she had to part with her holding to enable her to pay up during difficulties. She sent her family out to America. She was left with one boy, who was dumb. However, the money raised by selling her farm did not recover all the expenses of emigration.

When approval of her plan to emigrate became known, the agents took up her case in May 1848. There was no means of support available. It was recommended that £20 should be given to take her and her son to America.

The company's agents, John and Rowley Miller, had earlier set out their views on assisted passage to America, and this was an integral part of their plans to improve the estate. The passage money amounted to £4 10s. 6d., and not everyone could pay.

It was said that farms on the estate should be enlarged. There was never a greater opportunity to improve the estates in County Londonderry. The smallholders were frightened at the spectacle of the potato becoming extinct. The Drapers' Company suggested political orthodoxy, which pointed to the famine as a means and an opportunity to restore the Irish economy and society to more manageable proportions. This was the view of the landed elite.

In the south of County Londonderry lived other main landholders – a situation that obtained in the winter of 1846/7, when the effects of the famine were experienced quite sharply. The 3rd Marquess of Londonderry's estate at Magherafelt also experienced great hardship. Both John Andrews (agent to the County Down estate) and Andrew Spottiswood (agent to the Londonderry estate) informed Lord Londonderry about the state of the peasants on the Magherafelt estate, where the small tenants were said to be starving. Ideally, some sort of employment for the poor had to be found. Confirmation of this came in greater detail from the Magherafelt agent in January 1847. He said that the poor were suffering from both sickness and destitution. The new Relief Act was not yet in operation. The workhouse was closed for a while before it increased in numbers. As the number of the poor dropped, places became available.

Lord Londonderry was criticized in the press in January and February 1847 for his alleged neglect of the tenantry on his many Ulster estates. The *Londonderry Standard* said that he did not contribute more than necessary. Londonderry's response was not much different from that of the Drapers' Company – to provide assistance to the most in want. Andrews assured Londonderry that his thinking was along the same lines. The needy, even before Londonderry's letter, continued to want and perish in their hovels in Ulster.

The crisis continued to deepen, and provoked another County Londonderry landowner, George Dawson of Castledawson, to put on record his own reaction to the plight of the paupers, which greatly distressed him. He could think of nothing else but the poor condition of the people. If prices made it impossible to support a family, he welcomed women and children crying in the streets, hoping that someone might save them from starvation. So great was their plight that they often fell over when food hit their stomachs. Dawson's kindness was acknowledged later in the crisis, when other landlords took action as he had. He talked about the tyranny of the Irish landlords. He said that he had encouraged his tenantry to be loyal to him. He established a brick factory and gave 100,000 bricks to the poorest tenants so that they could improve their hovels.

Charity in County Londonderry took the form of landlords contributing to local relief and receiving aid from relief committees. The company also donated £125 of the £709 collected by the Aghadowey and Agivey subscription list.

Local response to the famine is not altogether clear. The Reverend John Brown, the minister at Aghadowey, said that he was most unwilling to give offence to any landlord, and most of all to one such as the Marquess of Waterford, in the south of Ireland. He thought that the meeting should request him to attend to the paupers on his estates. However, the number of the poor continued to rise as the famine started to bite. Lord Waterford had been verbally attacked and this ran counter to his reputation as an 'improving' landlord.

Lord Waterford appears to have been responsive to the local criticism of Lord Londonderry, which appeared in a newspaper article. At Christmas 1846 he wrote from his Waterford estate to John Barre Beresford, his agent in County Londonderry, to say that he had received a letter stating that £300 was sufficient to give to the poor. He said that he had received some sad reports from the clergy, who said that relief should be immediate. He had established soup kitchens in the different parishes in which he had property.

Further money was to be used to help support the soup kitchens in the nine parishes where he held land. He said that the greatest obstacle would come from the destitute on his estate. He said that the clergy of the different parishes should be informed of his intentions. The ideal situation was that landlords and clergy would work in harmony with one another for the benefit of the tenantry. Any local dissatisfaction with landlord performance continued to be voiced by the Reverend J. Jackson. Writing from Ballinderry to the Relief Commission in March 1847, he lamented that every one of the landlords were non-resident and the population consisted of cottiers and small farmers. There was no mention of the foundation of any committee from which he could expect help in the care of the poor. In conjunction with the rector's family, he had made great advances since the beginning of the year. Relief and money were also raised amongst his friends.

The Reverend Mitchell Smyth wrote as chairman of the Garvagh Relief Committee echoing Reverend Jackson's regret at the dearth of leadership which a landlord needed in order to provide for a stricken region. He asked the Relief Commission for the necessary instructions as soon as possible. This land was the poorest and most destitute in the county. There were no resident landlords and no industry or public works to occupy the people.

Many submissions were made on behalf of the relief committee, and these provide an opportunity to reckon not only the role of the landlords but also that of clergy in the management of relief until the main responsibility passed to the union in 1847. At Portstewart there were no less than eight clerics, who raised a total of £421. There were other acts of charity carried out by the clergy – for instance in the form of pleas on behalf of their commissioners. The Reverend Jackson was praised for his efforts at relief in his Ballinderry parish. He received no reply from the Relief Commissioners. He followed up a week later, begging for an increase in the food allowance in his district for those who were destitute and who were suffering from dysentery. Three weeks later, having still received no reply, he renewed his plea and stated that a man and his wife had died one night, probably from starvation. The Reverend William Hughes, Church of Ireland minister of the parish of Aghadowey, near Limavady, wrote in November 1846 that great distress was now beginning to be felt in that place by the labourers and cottier class. The Reverend John P. Hewitt referred to the collectors for the poor in a meeting taking place in the two meeting houses and the Roman Catholic chapel. He said that distress was increasing every day. He judged that the distress did not prevail in other places but that destitution in general was great and their need urgent. He referred to the soup kitchen dispensing one hundred gallons of soup daily, supplying 228 families, consisting of upwards of 1,180 persons. The workhouse at Magherafelt was full up, and it was not designed to cope with tragedies like this great famine.

The replies of the Presbyterian clergy active in local relief work obeyed the will of God. The Reverend Adam Boyle, minister of Bovedy near

Kilrea, recorded events that took place in the ninety-second year of his age. He had a tremor of the hand, and he could only be sure of Christ's suffering on the Cross. He said that a dereliction of duty is often followed by judgment. They shared the united supplications so that relief would be brought about by prayer. At Castledawson, the Presbyterian minister, Reverend William J. Radcliff, inserted a memoir in the sessions minute book in September 1848 which indicated the extent of the fever. The winter was full of calamity. Hunger was everywhere visible. The people changed from a diet of potatoes to a diet of Indian meal, and they went down with a most wasting dysentery. Relief committees were established to help the situation. Donations were made by the clergy and flock of the Roman Catholic Church, the Church of Ireland and the Presbyterian Church. It was wearisome to spend day after day on relief committees and to see at first hand the miserable state of the people. All joy seemed to disappear from the people's faces.

Hewitt's reference to the Magherafelt workhouse accommodation in March 1847 was a strong indication of the accelerating pace at which the disaster was taking place. In early January none of the five workhouses serving the countryside had failed. At Coleraine and Magherafelt there was no great pressure on the workhouses, even though at Magherafelt over 250 paupers had been admitted in the previous month. At Londonderry it was noted that additional buildings were now in the course of erection. At Ballymoney there was the possibility of not being able to cope. The commissioners called the attention of the guardians to their paupers. There were offers to cooperate in providing additional workhouse accommodation. By the beginning of February, the Ballymoney workhouse had exceeded its capacity; and this was also the case in Coleraine and Magherafelt by early March 1847. At Magherafelt the statistics show that over 400 had fallen back upon the workhouse in December and January. This was further evidence of the distress described by the local clergyman.

Winter came. Overcrowding spread. By the beginning of March, Londonderry had only two spare places in its capacity of 800. Only Newtown Limavady continued to fall short of its total in periods of severity. The number in each workhouse from December 1846 to May 1847 dropped; only Coleraine and Ballymoney remained overcrowded. Coleraine had a limit of 700 in December 1846, but accommodated 779 in May 1847.

The crisis of the spring months went away slowly, only to resume in the autumn with the third appearance of the potato blight in 1847. By December 1847 the workhouse population exceeded that of the corresponding month in 1846. In Magherafelt the workhouse population increased by twenty-five per cent to 908; in Ballymoney by twenty-six per cent to 706; and in Coleraine by thirty-one per cent to 731. Londonderry's 914 was the highest figure, thirty-seven per cent higher than the previous year's total.

At the same time, the fever hit the workhouses. By the autumn of 1848 there were only a small number of poor in County Londonderry's workhouses compared with 1847. The limit at Coleraine was 960; at Ballymoney it was 750. The many that fell victim to the famine began to assume great proportions in the winter of 1847/8. Between July and September 1847 the total increased from forty-one to 136 and peaked in late December of the same year at 171. The Reverend William J. Radcliff exhorted the authorities to halt the starvation. He wrote that the winter that succeeded 1847 was a terrible one of fever. From January 1847 to January 1848, fifty-two persons died – one every week. On two separate occasions there were three funeral meetings in the graveyard at the same time. On two other occasions he saw two coffins brought together in the same cart. He wished that he would never again witness such a spectacle and that God would save County Londonderry.

As well as the intensity of the fever, one of the most striking features of the workhouse population in Ulster in the years 1847–8 was the large number of children at starvation point. In early 1847 there were 16,349 children aged under fifteen in Ulster workhouses – forty-nine per cent of the total population of 33,238 souls. This figure climbed to fifty-three per cent by July. The proportion of children under the age of fifteen in the Munster workhouse at the same time was forty-one per cent; in Leinster, 42.5 per cent; and in Connaught forty per cent. This was the rule since before the time of the famine, as a result of social distress. The *Coleraine Chronicle* reported in September 1844 that one William Thompson was accused of leaving his wife and children, sending them as burdens into the union workhouse. There was an influx of starving children, which was noted by Edward Senior, the Poor Law inspector in whose northern district stood all the county's workhouses, except for that of Londonderry city. Parents dumped their children into the workhouses, much to his concern. This was evident in March 1849 when the Select Committee on the Poor Law (Ireland) asked the guardians to spend more energies on the poor who had been deserted by their families. They offered rewards, and very often parties arrived from districts in Scotland and England.

By the following month, April 1849, Senior circulated a letter to some unions, including Ballymoney, urging them to send emigrants and any able-bodied inmates, especially females. In this way the death rate was reduced in the electoral division. The guardians of Londonderry and Coleraine addressed the problem by reuniting parents with their children and arranging emigration as one family. Approval was obtained by 1849 by each of these boards of guardians for the transportation to Canada of sixty-four paupers. In the case of Londonderry and Coleraine, fifty-six emigrated to Quebec.

The power of the Poor Law guardians to proceed with these schemes was increased in 1848 by the Monsell amendment to the Poor Law Act. After this, workhouse-assisted passage increased for some years. The number emigrating was 5,000 paupers annually, but the problem of orphans increased in the workhouses. Landlords assisted in emigration more than the Poor Law guardians. The countryside surrounding the five workhouses in County Londonderry sent only 109 female orphans to Australia in a scheme in which over 4,100 parentless children, from workhouses throughout Ireland, sailed to start new lives in Australia. The project was undertaken by the Poor Law Commissioners in close collaboration with the Colonial Office in London. They saw it as an opportunity to improve the population in the Australian colony. Here males outnumbered females by over three to one.

The exercise had to be abandoned in 1850 after only two years, following accusations about the immoral behaviour of orphans from the Belfast workhouse on board the *Earl Grey.*

The workhouse records show that the Londonderry and Coleraine guardians pitied one Letty Harper, a widow. The minutes also record that the orphan girls going to Australia were brought on board in clothing prepared for them. The chairman and vice-chairman tried to make sure that the paupers were suitable for emigration to Australia.

The guardians at Coleraine and Londonderry assisted the passage of the orphans and their 'mother'. This was a means of addressing the problem not only for the orphans but also for additional people in the Ulster workhouse population. There was a preponderance of females amongst the adult population in the workhouses of the province, and this was particularly evident in County Londonderry. By the middle of 1848 the ratio amongst able-bodied adults in the Ulster workhouses was nearing three females for every one male. The ratio in the other provinces was close to two females for every one male. By November 1848 the percentage of females in the Ulster workhouses was seventy-seven per cent of the able-bodied adult inmates. This compares with sixty-six per cent in November, sixty-seven per cent in Connaught and seventy-two per cent in Leinster. The number of females in the workhouses of County Londonderry during the same period was eighty per cent compared with seventy-four per cent in December 1846. The preponderance of females may well have been associated with the phenomenon of emigration from Ulster before and during the famine. One member of a family would emigrate – usually the man – and he would prepare the way for the rest of his family to join him.

Londonderry was the busiest emigration port for the Gaels sailing the Irish Sea to North America – mainly to Philadelphia and New York. The passenger books of the emigration agents, J. & J. Cooke, provide evidence of the business of the port. Emigrants also came from County Tyrone, County Antrim and, above all, County Donegal. In May 1851, statistics recording the extent of emigration began to be collected. The annual average rate of emigration from County Londonderry between 1851 and 1855 was reckoned at 3,168. Londonderry therefore had a wide hinterland. In one year, some 12,385 poor set sail for Quebec, New York and Philadelphia.

The Irish travelled to the New World in relative comfort. The situation changed when the first cases of typhus and cholera (diseases dreaded by the famine ships) were reported in the late summer of 1847. Three hundred and sixty passengers arrived at Grosse Island and many were sick. One ship was lost – the English ship *Exmouth*, which had foundered off the coast of Scotland, losing most of its 240 passengers. In 1848, the following year, there loomed another deadly spectre – the spectre of the coffin ship. Vere Foster travelled incognito on board the *Washington* and reported his findings to the House of Commons at Westminster in 1851.

On 5 December the *Belfast Newsletter* and other local papers carried the headline 'Horrible Catastrophe – Seventy-Two Lives Lost by Suffocation in a Storm'. The *Londonderry*, sailing from Sligo to Liverpool, had put into port at Londonderry to shelter from the storm. The steerage passengers (who had begun their journey as cargo in the ship) had suffered a good deal when the crew had crammed them into the hold when the storm blew up. The sight of the ship anchoring in Londonderry was a sorry spectacle for the citizens.

Alexander Lindsay, the mayor, and several local magistrates, were in attendance. The scene in the steerage area was perhaps as awful a sight as could be witnessed: seventy-two men lay dead, and women and children lay piled four-deep. This presented a ghastly spectacle, for most of the dead had suffered suffocation.

There was a disturbing human and cargo traffic which was evident at the port of Londonderry during the famine, when there was no means of employment.

Sir Robert Ferguson, as Lord Lieutenant of the county, relayed his reports to Dublin regarding the great failure of the potato crop. He referred to the railway construction and associated land reclamation that had been undertaken. In 1845, the railway was about to take passengers, and this would provide internal transport from one end of the county to the other. Shortly after this communication, Ferguson made it his business to apply pressure on the Dublin & Enniskillen, and Londonderry to Coleraine railways. The company informed the relief committee that a very large number of men could be immediately employed on Londonderry lines, which embraced a large district. The Coleraine line was deserving of mention not only as a source of immediate employment, but for the utilization of 22,000 acres of very fair land, which would be reclaimed in the construction of the line between Coleraine and Londonderry. The construction difficulties associated with land reclamation provided a number of jobs until the line was opened in 1832–3. The line initially ran from Limavady to Coleraine. Later, a bridge was built across the River Bann at Coleraine. It opened up the county to unbroken rail communication with Belfast and beyond.

There is much controversy in speculating when the famine ended. In the southern parts of County Londonderry some communities supported the view that after 1847 things started to improve. The Reverend Samuel Montgomery, Church of Ireland rector of Ballynascreen, wrote in his register that the crop of potatoes during the autumn of 1847 was only diseased in a small measure.

In the spring of 1848 many potatoes had been planted. George Dawson expanded on his assessment. In writing to Sir Thomas Fremantle, chairman of the board of guardians, in November 1847, he let it be known that County Londonderry had a most abundant harvest in everything, including potatoes. The sown potatoes were of the highest quality. However, they were beginning to show signs of not keeping. It was not like the disease of the previous year, but more similar to that of 1846. He said that he had not been called upon by the poor and that he could walk about quite at liberty when the famine was at its height.

The expectation of better times was not entirely reflected in the numbers applying for admission to the workhouse during 1848. The five workhouses serving County Londonderry remained under continual pressure in the early months of 1848, and there was a seasonal fall in numbers by June, as the weather and employment opportunities improved.

The fever spread amongst the population, whose resistance to the disease was weakened after the autumn of 1845. This was one of the post-blight consequences which Lord Londonderry's Magherafelt agent addressed in a communication to His Lordship in the October of 1847. He said that he had been making every arrangement in his power to enforce payment, but he regretted that the failure of the potato crop had placed the smallholders on the estate in an adverse position, and they had suffered very severely for some months from sickness. He said that there were about 150 cases of fever in the hospital sheds attached to the workhouse, where the inmates were daily increasing.

There is no evidence that tenants of Londonderry's Magherafelt estate were evicted, although there were evictions in his other Ulster estates – mainly in County Donegal but also in County Antrim. Cahal Dallat reported that the agent for the Garron Tower estate was removed from his holding.

In 1850, a fellow landlord, George Dawson, commented that the tenants were being incited to agitation. If it had not been for Lord Londonderry's foolishness there might not have been any trouble. He continued to make his concerns public on the possibility of the revolt of the poor. In the same letter, Dawson expressed his view that it was easier to keep a good tenant than to evict a bad one.

There is no record of eviction on the Drapers' Company estate. The agent's letter book, however, continued to record the emigration of the poor. By 1849 the company had spent almost £950 to assist over 400 tenants to emigrate. The other London Companies adopted the policy of clearance by stealth: the Fishmongers' estate at Ballykelly provided for some sixty tenants to emigrate with their families, and the Grocers' estate nearby also contributed to the remaining eight families in the period 1849–51, helping to bring about the consolidation of the farmers.

The numbers of the poor being given relief in the County Londonderry workhouses in the latter half of 1848 and in 1849 show how painfully delayed was an overall improvement. All five workhouses had to cope with further inmates in September 1848 and June 1849. A rise in the numbers of the poor during the late autumn of 1848 would have been expected; but there was a slight decline in the population from March to June 1849, when a bigger decline might have been expected. The memory of the blight years was to be long-standing.

George Dawson had earlier written panic-stricken accounts from his Castledawson estate. He was reluctant to condemn the poor and he detailed the times of the 1849 harvest. In comparison with the previous years' crops the results were disappointing, but on the whole the earth teemed with produce. As yet there was not the slightest appearance of disease in the potatoes, but he said that it was too soon to speak with

110

any confidence. In 1848 the deadly blight appeared on 3 August. He predicted a lot of human misery. The county's landlords were in a continuously expectant frame of mind, but this was not reflected by the tenantry.

Henry Keenan had some twelve acres of land at Ballyscullion, on the Bruce estate. He described the situation in a letter he wrote that same month, July 1849, to his brother at Baltimore, Maryland. There was a note of hopelessness in the years succeeding the famine, and this is evident from the remarks of a man who had been entirely devoid of the means of supporting himself or his family and who now feared the worst.

He had been unwell from November to May, but he thanked God that he was recovering. He had seven sons at his side with him, and times were worsening. He felt there was no chance of recovery from the disease. He wanted to know in another letter how his sons should earn their living.

Keenan's solution – emigration – was favoured by the landlords in his locality, but for different reasons. When statistics about emigration became available the rate of emigration from County Londonderry in the five-year period 1851–5 was put at 3,168. By this time (1851), the population of the county had decreased by 15.5 per cent of its 1841 total. It fell from 221,174 to 192,022 in 1851. The most significant decline in manufacturing was in County Coleraine, in the parishes of Macosquin, Aghadowey and Lamlagh, particularly in the barony of Loughinsholin. In other parishes the drop was upwards of twenty-five per cent.

It is difficult to calculate the number that died during the course of the famine, but it was said that there was one million dead. The 1851 census indicated that there had been 25,883 deaths in County Londonderry. The annual average number of deaths between the years 1842 and 1845, before the famine took root, was 1,723. The best evidence available is that there were approximately 1,000 deaths for the years 1846–50 in County Londonderry. Regardless of the statistics, the evidence of the observers, made up of clergymen, relief-committee personnel, tenants and even the landlords themselves, was used to compile an account of County Londonderry during the famine. Records show a picture of difficulties which the potato blight imposed upon the greater proportion of the population.

Chapter 8

The Great Hunger in County Monaghan

County Monaghan lies in the south of Ulster. Like most of Ulster it did not suffer the extreme poverty of the west of Ireland. It was one of the most prosperous regions in the province. The famine impact in the 1840s showed that County Monaghan occupied a traditional location between Ulster and the rest of Ireland. The population had to undergo its ordeal and indications show that the South Ulster borderlands had valuable economic features in keeping with Malthusian policies of the 1830s and 40s.

John Donovan's outburst against poverty, voiced in County Donegal in the early 1830s, was a typical reflection of Ireland's troubles. He said that in rural Ireland the Irish peasant found himself without enough land to support himself and others. He became anti-Malthusian, and he was against sowing the soil with Celtic crops. However, the potato was still regarded as the main means of sustenance. The measures would never succeed in Ulster or County Monaghan. The present state of things was a situation of general destitution.

Population is the most sensitive way of judging the effects of the Great Hunger. Population had implications for pressure on the land, housing conditions, landholding circumstances, land revenue and landscape. All of this indicates what conditions prevailed at local level in the 1840s.

South Ulster (Monaghan and Cavan) contained some of the most heavily populated areas in Ireland in 1841. Freeman's computation of population density indicates an extensive belt of countryside running from South Cavan through Monaghan into Armagh and the parishes of North Louth, which contained over 400 persons. This density is reflected along the west coast of Ireland. Monaghan entered the nineteenth century with a large rural population pressure compared with the pressure on the land in the west of Ireland. Land in the west was not as good as in Monaghan and it was more remote. In County Cavan in 1841 there were some of the most extensively overpopulated districts in the country.

Overpopulation is a much abused term. The population/resources relationship had been unbalanced in Monaghan. Farms had become minuscule and there were too many people with limited or no access to land. Few had access to non-farm incomes. In the south-east the manufacture of goods was in hot retreat. This left a huge population of landless unemployed. The industrialization of the linen trade, separated Monaghan's experience of the famine from that of the other Ulster counties, particularly Armagh, in the 1840s.

The population of County Monaghan in 1841 was 200,442, and most of it lived off the countryside. This represents an annual rural density of fifty-eight persons per one hundred acres (370 persons per square mile). The most desolate acres were in the south and east and middle of the county. The barony of Farney in the south had some of the most highly populated rural areas. The lowest densities were to be found in the mountains in the north-west. One quarter of the townlands in Monaghan had extremely high population densities of more than seventy-six persons per one hundred acres. Many of the townlands in the baronies of Farney and Dartrey had densities amounting to between 600 and 1,100 persons per square mile – one of the most overcrowded regions in Europe. At townland level there were local pressures on the population coming from the land at a time when the farms were quite large. Such areas were rare in County Monaghan. On the other hand, Drumbracken had a population density of 216 persons per square mile in 1985. The population in 1985 is given for comparison reasons and to put into perspective the conditions in pre-famine times. The contrast in the situation then and now shows the dire straits the people were in and why they wanted to emigrate. In trying to understand events on the land, social conditions and demographic conditions in 1841, two different dimensions may be looked at. First there were the owners of the land holding both small and large estates; and secondly there were the occupiers of the land – tenants, farmers, cottiers and other poor inhabitants of the countryside.

The landowners' estates had some sort of immigrant policy, which operated to a greater or lesser extent depending upon the solvency of the owner in the running of his property.

Management of sectors of land by owners in the pre-famine years is a most important factor in understanding the nature of the demographic and social problems. For larger proprietors, estates' officers employing personnel such as agents, bailiffs and clerks applied a range of services in an effort to gain the most efficient use of the land. The ultimate objective was to squeeze as much income out of the land as possible. Farmers were organized by means of leases and other contractural obligations imposed by right of possession. Some owners had much less management experience and made only occasional contributions to the running of their estates. There were long intervals, perhaps during the sale of property, when surveys of the land were taking place.

At a general level, in theory, the imposition of controls had the effect of controlling the number of farms, the sale of farms and the passing on of farms to the next generation. The subletting of land to cottier tenants was also controlled. But the situation remained static as a result of mismanagement, lack of interest in the tenants and indifference towards suffering. In all cases the estates, a legally recognized division of the land, containing a number of occupiers, provide an important account of the situation. It was important to have respect for Monaghan's population in the early mid-nineteenth century.

Estates exceeding 2,000 acres in County Monaghan were carefully planned out. Estates like those in County Monaghan had officers – for example, at Carrickmacross for the Shirley and Bath estates, in Glaslough, and also the Leslie estates. The larger estates were mostly situated in the lowlands of County Monaghan. Most of the smaller properties were of less than 500 acres. They probably did not have a permanent administrative presence beyond a solicitor's office in the town, in which transactions such as the payment of rent could take place. The majority of the smaller estates in mid-nineteenth-century Monaghan had addresses outside the county. For example, in 1858 eighty-eight out of 154 properties of 100–500 acres were owned by persons not living in the countryside, but in the neighbouring counties or further afield. Of the twenty-eight largest estates in Monaghan only seven were non-resident – Lord Bath lived in Wiltshire and Viscount Templeton lived in Down. Many of the residents spent some time in England – for example, Shirley of Carrickmacross.

The ordinary Celts or Gaels lived in their thousands in cabins scattered across the hills. It was they that carved up the farms and fields which covered the landscape, and they had a central role in the social and economic processes which went with the making of the problems of rural Monaghan in pre-famine decades. They operated within the bounds of the estate. The records of the Shirley, Leslie and Dawson estates reflect this. From the Shirley estate, many records exist from before the famine. There was talk of subdivision and subletting in 1843. There were regulations about the keeping of goats, which destroyed the privacy of the poor. There were petitions made by the Irish tenants to their landlords on a wide variety of matters. Unlike the Hillsborough estate a great many of the estates in Monaghan were small and scattered, and had no better use than the yearly collection of rent. The occupiers of the land were left alone. There were many cases of great poverty in the pressure areas in the mid-nineteenth century.

The Devon Commission reported in 1845. It said that significant differences in the bigger and smaller Monaghan estates had come to light. Tenants agreed that the landholding on the larger estates was a good choice, with rents and valuations more acceptable. Rents on the larger estates were seen to be close to the Poor Law valuation of the land and in some cases below it. The Shirley estate was exceptional, with rents estimated to be twenty-one per cent above the official valuation. Smaller estates, often with an absentee owner, were the least desirable from the tenants' point of view. There were pre-famine evictions in County Monaghan, and these were reported to the commission. Lord Wingfield held absentee land. Patrick Murphy, a tenant, said that he did not know where the landlord and landlady were. He had a relation in Dublin and he called at Cork Abbey, but they were not there. He had heard that the Colonel was in Connaught and the landlady away from home.

The Devon Commission provided a look at the landholding system at a particular moment in time. The landlords' structure underlay the demographic dilemma of the 1840s. It was the product of two or more generations of mismanagement. A broad picture of the landlord structure emerged, but there were many exceptions. In 1835 the new heir to the Rathwell estate of over 2,000 acres reaped great rewards for the attention to his property. The landlord had to evict fifty-two families who were mere cottiers in whom he had no interest. Many were not known by name to Mr Rathwell or his agent. They were known as undertenants and they lived in hovels. Cottiers on a nearby farm lived in a ditch and never paid rent. A tenant of the estate said that the landlord had lived in Nice for many years. There was confirmation by the agent, who said that Mr Rathwell's usual residence from 1836 to 1842 was well known in County Meath, but that he occasionally occupied the manor house on his estate in County Monaghan. In 1842 he went to live in Italy for health reasons. The agent lived in Dublin, and said that he visited the Monaghan estate six to eight times a year.

The Lucan estate had 170 tenants in the mid-eighteenth century, but this figure later increased. This policy of land division was facilitated in the early years by the expansion of the linen industry. Growing flax, spinning and weaving in the late eighteenth century provided the major landlords with the possibility of stable rents in the future. They encouraged occupiers to fragment their inheritance of land. By the late eighteenth century there were low-profile management policies in regard to periods of economic expansion. Corn was at a high price and textiles kept both tenants and proprietors happy. It was only when prices declined in the 1830s that fearful Malthusian policies began to loom.

Until 1828 the Shirley estate, which the landlord only occasionally visited, had a querulous management regime. Tenants complained of poor conditions under various agents. In 1843, the newly appointed agent, William Steuart Trench supported their positions. There was little interference with the tenants' occupation of the land, in spite of warnings of a dangerous multiplicity of holdings on the estate. In a survey as far back as 1789, it was pointed out that the tenants had increased in great measure in the last fifty years. They might reproduce at the same rate for the next fifty years, and the situation would greatly change. The difficulty was that employment had to be found for these increased numbers. Another survey pointed out that it would not be profitable to work the land without sweeping away the present population. The farmers were now called upon to change the status quo. Policy did not change with the coming of the Poor Law. A landlord named Mitchell attended to the poor of his estate in 1843, and he openly encouraged subdivision of the farms in 1839. He threatened to evict a tenant who refused to give a portion of his land to his son. Trench took over in 1843 and attempted to impose order in the affairs of the property. He became very unpopular by removing cottiers.

In the decades before the famine one could talk of a balancing act or a series of compromises between owners of land. This throws ultimate light on the eventual shape of things. The landowners, the tenants and land agents worked together. Agents with other land personnel were powerful in situations where the landowner was non-resident, and often their advice and experience were essential to the running of the property on a day-to-day basis. Agents represented the interests of the landowners, but in many cases they also represented their own personal interests through managing leases for favourites. On the Shirley estate, extreme changes were imposed on the tenants. The tenants tried to outwit the agents, so that the proprietor could not obtain his rent. Landowners were called 'Your Honour'. A study of the crown rents in County Roscommon explains the extent of aid on the property. They show the effect that the local tenantry had on the ability of the various agents to understand the complexities of tenurial arrangements. In 1847 there were 2,647 people, in 591 cottier families, on the Shirley estate, many of them tenants or undertenants.

The Fourth Class was the lowest category of dwelling. In 1841 these dwellings were generally without windows. The classification was often left to the discretion of the local constabulary. The poorest houses in the parish of Aghnamullen in 1836 were almost beyond description – very low and open, ill built, some built of sods, some of stone without mortar, thatched, damp and smoky. In terms of house quality, Monaghan was about average nationally. It did not have the same problems as the west of Ireland, where housing shortage was a major problem. Monaghan was part of a great region that stretched from South Leinster to North-East Ulster where twenty-four per cent of houses were in the Fourth Class. Within the county, the poorest houses were concentrated in the southernmost parishes. In the north, around Monaghan town, more than one third of houses were in the Fourth Class, but overall in the county less than a fifth of houses were in the Fourth Class category. The linen industry played an economic role in helping to relieve population pressures on the land and in improving the rudimentary condition of housing.

The Devon Commission evidence concerning Monaghan does not record as many harrowing tales as in regions like County Mayo, West Galway. The landless were not so numerous in Monaghan, which was mainly a county of smallholders. There was a considerable population of smallholders in some places, as in the west of the county. Unlike Leinster, whose landless population had a labour relationship with the farm population, the Monaghan cottier was in a dicey situation. Some were linked to the larger farms of the Monaghan area (which extended from Clones north-eastwards to Glaslough and the southern extremities of the county). There numbers were limited. The Devon Commission voted that the major farmers in the parish of Magheross should have forty acres. There were only about ten of these in the whole parish, each having from four to six cottiers. Many of the people were legacies of an earlier, more vibrant, rural textile economy on the Lucan estate in Castleshane, where there were eight mills. The cottiers were essential to the rent structure. One estate in North Armagh, whose rents were paid to the tenant farmers, amounted to one fifth of the rent of the estate. The agent on the Lucan estate reported that often a man had built his home on a corner of a four- or five-acre estate, then he had married the farmer's daughter and become his labourer.

On the Shirley estate, Trench tried to break a well-established tradition for small farms to help cottiers. In 1844, Owen Fitzpatrick pleaded to be allowed to keep his labourer, permitted by the previous agent. A thatched home had been built for him.

In a county such as County Monaghan, where small farms were dominant, employment opportunities for the landless population were extremely limited. The cottier families subsisted on whatever work they could find at home (or abroad, in some cases). According to the Ordnance Survey of 1835 there were in the south of County Monaghan a few patches of ground where cultivation had not been affected. Monaghan was therefore a highly labour-intensive landscape. By 1845 a great many of the cottiers were employed for two thirds of the year, according to the Devon Commission.

In 1841 the linen industry was well in decline in the county. By 1851 it virtually did not exist. This development was reflected in the disappearance during the famine of labourers, mostly from the spinning industry. In the 1851 census there were 24,687 women engaged in industry (mostly in spinning), and 3,400 men, mainly concentrated in the parishes of Central and West Monaghan. By 1851 the corresponding figures were 2,331 females to 1,283 men.

Small tillage holding was the main characteristic of the rural landscape in mid-nineteenth-century County Monaghan. The nature of the farms did not radically affect the overall pattern of smallholdings. The greatest concentration was to be found in the eastern districts of the county. More than a quarter of farm holdings in much of Farney, and around Monaghan and Clones town, were of less than five acres. Over three quarters of the holdings of the baronies of Farney and Cremorne were of less than fifteen acres – decidedly small farm regions.

There was great destitution in Ireland before the famine, and figures of paupers under care point to more direct evidence of the destitution in pre-famine Monaghan.

Trench's survey of the Shirley estate provides an insight into conditions prevailing over a large section of the county. Trench is hated in local folk memory. He was a land agent and wrote down his memoirs. His attitude to the poor generally ranged from contempt to racial arrogance. The report he wrote to Shirley, following his appointment in 1843, throws interesting light upon conditions on a large estate. He spent some months travelling on the estate, visiting the tenants' homes and other property. He was quite frank in his reactions to what he saw. He said that even in Ireland he had never witnessed such destitution. He noted that there were many tenants' homes where there were no windows or tables. He emphasized the connection between the economic depression, falling agricultural prices and the serious position of the tenantry. Fingers were pointed at the landlords. The tenantry upon his estate were in a state of poverty and depression, and the moral duty of the landlords should have been to relieve the destitution of their people.

The records of the Shirley estate show the grim reality of life for many desperate people in South Monaghan in the year before the famine. The number and range of the petitions are not only a reflection of the gathering storm, but also illustrate the welfare role which the estate played in the lives of the people in the mid-nineteenth century. As early as the 1840s many Irish sought relief in the form of concessions in rent arrears – for example, help in times of sickness. The most common requests were for blankets. This reflects the great poverty of the area, and is a universal indication of want, especially amongst the landless, in winter.

Deaths from the famine were appalling. In January 1844, Henry Magill of Carrickmaclin lived as a cottier with John Reburn and a family comprising a wife and four children. It had pleased God to afflict him with an ulcerous leg, which excluded him from labouring. He was one of those in need of blankets.

Anne McEneaney, whose pig had died, held two acres of land near Carrickmacross. In February 1844 she sought a blanket for her son, who was on his deathbed.

Francis McCabe of Peaste in December 1844 lived on his aunt's farm, and he was put to the expense of burying her. Her death had a traumatic effect. By bringing in the harvest he only earnt enough to enable him to clear his arrears of rent. He, his wife and two children had no peace of mind either day or night. They only had light woollen clothing, so they were suffering with cold.

Widows were also vulnerable: in January 1845, a woman complained that her husband was dying. She hoped that the authorities would give her some clothing to thwart the intense cold of the season.

The cottiers and smallholders were in a serious position in the early 1840s. In his report, Trench paid particular attention to the way the estate had pressurized the smaller tenants by establishing a system to make sure that rents were paid on time. Rents were kept up – little or no arrears accumulated at first – but the tenants in time grew poorer and poorer until they were unable to keep up the rent.

Peter Mahon was a typical farmer, farming three acres in the parish of Magheracloone, and he attacked problems at their grass roots in County Monaghan on the eve of the famine. He told the Devon Commission that if he obtained his land cheaply, it would keep him out of the workhouse. He survived in the summer season and was able to earn a decent wage. He bought some oats and made a little meal out of it, and in this way he supported himself. In 1841, people on his land had held ten acres, and they included eleven householders. His rents amounted to the price of the suit he wore.

Peter Mahon's little plot of land did not pay his rent, and he grew potatoes to feed him and his family. Despite the hardships, the presence of Peter Mahon in the same townland in 1858 is a reflection on his ability to survive.

The cottier population had nothing. They were often on the move, and only fleeting glimpses appear in the pages of the Devon Commission. The cottier wandered around, looking for a place to settle. Wherever sickness attacked, he was obliged to leave his hovel, and his family became beggars or went into the workhouse. Of the fifty-two cottiers who were evicted from the Rathwell estate in the late 1830s most went to America; some begged and some eked out a living elsewhere.

The situation in County Monaghan was critical and was affected by the Poor Law Act of 1838, which had an important effect upon the relationship between the land and the people. There were irregularities in property management in the previous half-century in the face of a declining economy. The effect of the Poor Law was to define the situation of the paupers. There was a large number of people whose property was at or below £4 valuation and, in times of recurring crisis, they would be supported by a new property tax. The landowners were alarmed. Properties with a limited number of poor relied upon the Poor Law divisions, which were responsible for paying the rates to support those paupers.

In County Monaghan, the boundary of the Bath estate, with a smaller cottier population than the Shirley estate, coincided with the Poor Law division. Estate valuations matched the boundaries of the new Poor Law Unions and electoral divisions. Those with a large number of poor kept quiet.

The Shirley estate was typical. The new policies introduced by Trench in 1843 ranged from the prohibition of subdivision and subletting through assisted emigration and ultimately to forced eviction. These measures were designed to reduce the rates burden upon the estates. Shirley's detailed survey of the cottiers on his estate between 1840 and 1847 was aimed at reducing his taxation liability.

The blight first appeared in the north of County Monaghan in 1845 –

it became the Great Hunger. To the farmers, cottiers and landowners it seemed like another crisis for the rural community. Many observers in the pre-industrial economy quickly realized that they might starve to death. The *Northern Standard* of 1 November echoed mutual concern. Calamity had come to the land as a result of the failure of the potato crop. The list of agricultural deaths is not very reliable, and some districts did not record any deaths in 1847. It is quite possible to obtain some individual data on the extent of the potato famine in the county from the estimates of the acreage of potatoes, when the beginnings of the blight started to appear. The potato acreage subsequently changed dramatically. The statistics do not give an accurate account of the crop, but they do indirectly point to failure. A large loss of potatoes in 1845 and 1846 would result in smaller planting the following season as a result of the shortage of seed. The 1847 acreage of potatoes in Scotstown, for example, was only fourteen per cent of what it was destined to be in 1851. The acreage in Carrickaslane, near Castleblayney, on the other hand, was five per cent. The greatest failures were in the north-east districts, in West Dartrey and the northern hills of Farney. There was an absence of potatoes, as found in the coroner's report in 1846 and 1847, which indicates that the potato famine was widespread.

Potatoes were planted in those districts where the smallholders and cottiers were most numerous. At the first hint of failure the poorer classes had little alternative but to try again. There were many large planted areas in the small-farm regions in 1847 in the east of Monaghan and around Carrickmacross. There was probably a high degree of failure in 1846. Eventually there was no seed left to plant. Great hardship appeared in West Dartrey and the north-east districts, where there were large numbers of landless labourers and where the potato crop failed miserably.

County Monaghan had some of the greatest losses in the whole of Ireland, but the situation was exceptional in Ulster. The decline in population between 1841 and 1851 in South Ulster reflects the transitional demographic status between Ulster and the north-west. Monaghan's population fell from more than 200,000 in 1841. Counties Monaghan and Cavan experienced the greatest agricultural decline in Ireland.

The counties in Ireland that experienced the greatest decline in population were Mayo (29.4%); Monaghan (29.2%); Cavan (28.4%); and Fermanagh (25.6%). In counties Antrim, Down, Londonderry, Donegal and Armagh the population fell by more than sixteen per cent. Tyrone lost eighteen per cent of its population. Within Monaghan twenty-five of the sixty electoral divisions had losses of more than thirty-five per cent, eleven of them losing more than forty per cent of their population in a decade. The heaviest losses in the western regions of the county were the densely populated districts of Cavan and Fermanagh. The small farms in the east of the county experienced little loss. Brogan, in the north-west mountainous region, was one of the few regions in Ireland with a one per cent decline in population. Half the townlands in the Shirley estate in Farney lost more than half of their populations. In the parish of Magheracloone the population fell from 9,012 to 5,141 between 1841 and 1851. In Magheross it fell from 11,447 to 6,419. The decline in housing perhaps reflects the changes across the countryside. The parish of Aghnamullen lost more than 1,000 houses in the decade of the famine. Some townlands had extraordinary declines – like Mullanary, outside Carrickmacross. Here the number of houses fell from 133 in 1841 to four in 1851.

One has to study the population losses: destitution is reflected in the rates of loss in each Poor Law Union. This was related to the population of the poor in the region, mainly comprised of the landless cottiers or smallholders with property valued at less than £4. Over one tenth of the property in the Monaghan Union was valued at less than £4. This is in contrast to between one quarter and one third in the Clones and Carrickmacross unions.

The crisis deepened and in the 1840s the rates were increased. Tenants in arrears and unable to pay rents were increasingly evicted by landowners with a view to lessening the burden on the rates, but this action put more pressure on the rates as the greater number of the poor were entering the workhouses. Shirley and other landowners tried to encourage cottiers to emigrate.

In County Monaghan, because of the small-farm situation, a great proportion of its tenantry were put under enormous pressure by the rates. Their small farms were classified just above the £4 level, and they were expected to contribute to the Poor Law rates. In the Castleblayney Union there were large numbers of tenants with farms valued at £4–5. They were under great pressure in 1847 with rates over three shillings in the pound. In January it was found impossible to collect the rate. In May the board attempted to lower the level of qualification for outdoor relief to below £4 to aid the great number of poor. In November it was becoming increasingly difficult to collect the rates. Many sold their crops and fled. Holdings valued between £4 and £5 were barely in the five- to fifteen-acre range in 1848.

Other areas also suffered a heavy decline. Many of these areas also contained large number of landless cottiers, renting land from the smallholders.

However, many smallholdings did not experience a high rate of population loss. Over one quarter of holdings in the south-eastern parish of Farney, for example, had less than five acres. In the north-west of the county, population loss was low in the decade 1841–51. Some farms were large, but low in value. The population could not emigrate. With their small farms they struggled through the Great Hunger.

Smallholders were desperate, and they were now under pressure from the blight on the one hand and rent and rates demands on the other. This is reflected in the appeal of Thomas and Mary Marron to Shirley's agent in February 1848. They said that they had always promptly paid the rent, but that they could not now pay. They said that the situation might improve at harvest time – they hoped for a good wheat crop together with oats, which they were about to sow.

The agricultural census that began in 1847 is almost certainly unreliable. Some districts show an increase in all types of holding between 1847 and 1851. For other districts there were no census returns. They serve to give an idea of the broad trends in farms and population in the years of the Great Hunger. There was a decline in holdings of less than fifteen acres, and it is impossible to show the nature of the population decline. The greatest losses between 1848 and 1851 occurred in the Monaghan Corridor and in the hills to the south of it. Five electoral divisions with about 500 holdings disappeared and accounted for half the total decline in the twenty divisions in the north of the county. The agricultural returns on holdings show the stability of the holdings in the light of the great social upheaval that had taken place. Holdings under fifteen acres declined by one quarter (amounting to 3,770 holdings) at a time when the population loss was 60,000 people. The reduction of the population as a result of the famine was greatest on the land. The average household size in Monaghan was 5.2 persons. The rate of holdings-to-population loss was close to 1:5. It can be assumed that smallholdings accounted for the decline. However, it is generally agreed that migration of families was significant during the famine.

In County Monaghan, as in the west of Ireland, the greatest number at risk came from the landless cottier class. Most of the coroners' reports show a sudden wave of deaths amongst landless families who spent the winter begging. This class was seriously depopulated by death and emigration. Ó Gráda records that a very high proportion of the emigrants to the United States were classed as labourers. Unlike in the far west of Ireland, County Monaghan's walking distance to parts of Dundalk and Newry made the voyage less daunting. The Shirley estate records for this period show that emigration from South Monaghan to ports like

Liverpool was quite usual.

There had also been traditionally a significant seasonal harvest migration out of the county into the Irish midlands and England. In 1835 an inquiry showed that hundreds of labourers were reported as dependent upon the English harvest. Not many appear to have left from the west and north of County Monaghan. Here there were large numbers of landless labourers. The 1831 census shows that over one third of all males aged twenty or over in the northern and western provinces were landless labourers. These districts had some of the highest population declines during the famine. Much of this loss is accounted for by high rates of mortality and migration amongst the landless people.

In the county in 1845, almost every parish experienced reductions by more than seventy per cent of houses in the Fourth Class category. In the parishes of Drumsnat, Kilmore, Donagh, Aghnamullen, Tullycorbet and Muckno there was a decline of more than eighty per cent. Nearly all the housing losses after 1851 were in the Fourth Class category. In the south of the county other categories of housing increased in the face of the huge losses in the poorest category. Some of these changes may be attributed to some houses being reclassified in the 1851 census. The elimination of the Fourth Class reflects the decline in the landless labourers class.

The poorest people in the western parishes of Ematris, Aghabog and Drummully experienced some of the worst conditions in the 1840s. Third Class houses in the census were marginally better in quality. There was a catastrophic decline in house prices after the famine. These changes affected most of rural Monaghan. The number of houses that existed is recorded in the Ordnance Survey (1835), but the estimates are unreliable for it is impossible to distinguish between dwellings and outhouses on the map. Where there were small groups, a range from the lowest to the highest number of protected homes was recorded. In the Dernamoyle townland, at least ten farmhouses can be seen on the map.

There were three landless houses in the Griffith's Valuation of 1835, and the rest was made up of a large number of landless houses. Between 1835 and 1841 there was a twenty-to-thirty-per-cent increase in the number of houses in the region. There were 411 houses in the nineteen townlands between 1841 and 1851 – a decline of fifty-three per cent, and there was a reduction of another twenty-five per cent between 1851 and 1858. In less than twenty years this small area in the west of Monaghan underwent a radical transformation in population and settlement.

In the parish of Ematris the majority of houses seem to have been cottier houses. In the Griffith's Valuation there were only six instances of holdings making up more than one allotment. This suggests that farms were divided very little in the preceding two decades. Farms and families had reached a degree of stability since 1841. There appear to have been only a few landholding houses in 1858. There was one left in the townland of Drumulla.

There was a huge decline in this townland from thirty-four to seven houses between 1841 and 1851, and these consisted mainly of cottier houses on the outskirts of the village of Rockcorry in the parish. There was a fifty-three-per-cent reduction in housing on high-density townlands, compared with thirty-three per cent for the whole parish. The continuity on the farms in the Griffith's Valuation suggests that the vast majority of houses that had disappeared were cottier houses.

The Ordnance Survey Memoirs for the parish of Ematris described the type of dwelling that was occupied by the poor in 1835: houses were made out of mud and divided into apartments, with small glass windows. The floor was made of earth with no ceiling, but only a roof of thatch. An area to one side served as a bedroom, and in the centre was a kitchen and dining room for the whole family. Comfort and cleanliness were not observed. It is impossible to describe the filth and destitution of these hovels and the enclosures around them. Families were large and the children huddled around the fire.

A large number of homes in the western parts of the county were affected by the decline of the linen industry. This was one of the largest flax-growing areas in Monaghan, and the soil was deep and damp. In 1835 there could be seen the ruins of extensive bleachfields around the region. Before the decline in the linen industry, spinning wheels and looms occupied an important place in the hovels, and they helped the householders to pay their rent. The plight of many of the poor is exemplified in the inquest of Mary Ann McDermott of Killeevan in March 1847. It was proposed that her mother and children should go to the workhouse or 'poor home', as they had no means of living except by begging. For the past fortnight she and her children had been in desperate straits. They had only a little gruel to eat at night, and this meal was collected during the day. Upon returning home on Friday Mary had suddenly taken ill. The doctor found in her stomach some greens of a coarse or bad kind. There was a quantity of raw turnip – probably the rind of the vegetable.

The distressed world of the Monaghan cottier was described in the inquest of Paul Murphy from the parish of Clontibret in February 1847.

The bedclothes of the deceased consisted of an old single blanket to shield him from the cold. His diet had been boiled turnips with meal and water. Often he would go a day without eating. His daughter slept on the floor of the hovel and had no bedclothes.

Coroners' reports were not made except in cases of sudden or unusual death. During the famine there was little that could be done about the great numbers of deaths which were the result of the famine. The cause of death was often simply 'destitution'.

In Magheracloone, in March 1847 local ministers insisted on having an inquest into the death of a cottier. His family had been living at the back of a ditch and they gave evidence that many people had met with sudden death in this parish as a result of destitution. The number of deaths in the parish had risen sharply in the previous seven or eight weeks. Deaths of many completely destitute people were occurring almost unnoticed by the more healthy inhabitants. Some days before his death the deceased and his family had been obliged to move from the ditch where they were living. He had used the fact that his daughter was ill to seek admission to the hospital, but admission was refused. When they found the deceased, he lay dead in an open field. A short distance away sat his wife and child, exposed to the elements. Witnesses said that the family had had to face the weather for three days and nights.

The decline in population in the barony of Farney is reflected in living conditions and estate policies in the area. The Bath estate appears to have adopted stringent controls as it entered the nineteenth century, and these controls seem to have remained the same on the Shirley estate.

When the rates were changed in the Carrickmacross Union in the later 1840s there was considerable opposition from the tenants of the Bath estate. Lord Bath resisted having to support what appeared to be Shirley paupers. The estate contained 18,000 people in 1841, and about sixteen per cent were cottiers. As early as May 1838, when the Poor Law was introduced, a letter from Lord Lismore mentioned Shirley's anxiety about the large number of poor tenants. He proposed to set up a 'sinking fund' to provide for 'useless' tenants. Trench was appointed in 1843, and he embarked upon a policy restricting any further subdivision of the holdings on the estate.

Laurence Levins was a cottier who felt the effects of the new policies. In March 1845 he was looking for a place to settle. His fate was cast for there was not a cabin to shelter him. His cousin, George, appealed to his landlord, who took his distressed state into consideration and generously offered him a site to build upon.

Trench's principal policy was one of assisted emigration. He wanted to pay the passage of the poorest tenants to America and thus reduce the burden upon his estate.

In July 1843, Francis Segreff pleaded that he had been a cottier for many years, and he had laboured honestly. For this, Mr Mitchell promised him a share in his estate. He wanted to build a small house for shelter for himself and his helpless family. He hoped that as his reputation was good, he would be granted permission. Trench refused his request, but an offer of assistance to America was accepted.

Between 1843 and the end of the blight the estate directly assisted more than 1,500 persons to emigrate. This was a controversial undertaking in Ireland generally. It was supported by the landless establishment. The local newspaper in County Monaghan was the *Northern Standard.* It was greatly in favour of emigration. It commented on 27 March 1847 that emigration was a great safety valve. If Monaghan had a population that was unmanageable, it would be in their interests to provide the tenants with the means to survive in those parts where there was room for expansion.

Shirley's emigrants were given their fares to America, and in many cases were provided for on the voyage. It is likely that others were assisted by having their arrears of rents written off upon the surrender of their holdings and the destruction of their hovels. The first emigrations from the Shirley estate preceded the famine by some years, but they intensified at the height of the famine. Between 1847 and 1849 hundreds were assisted off their estates, including about 150 who were sent to South America in 1849. There is evidence, in the petitions to the estate, of a growing need on the part of the tenants to emigrate. During the famine the urgency of the crisis changed the emphasis from cajolement to barefaced eviction. *The Nation* reported in September 1849 that Shirley had served notice of his intention to evict 245 people. The guardians of the Carrickmacross Union were already making provision for shelter of Shirley's 1,225 paupers. The 1,700 paupers at the Carrick workhouse in 1851 trebled the number in the other County Monaghan grounds that belonged to the Shirley estate.

Many others went to America without assistance. The difference between those who had assisted passage and those who did not was that subsidies assisted those tenants who were impoverished. According to Trench, in 1843 there were tenants who had no resources to emigrate. The population of Shirley's estate fell by over 8,000 between 1841 and 1851 – a decline of eighteen per cent – and this was attributed to his emigration policy. The repercussions of this policy went far beyond those who were able to make it to the New World. The assisted emigrants represented the creation of a pool of poor people. The result was a chain of emigration from districts in the county. The difference in population between the Shirley estate and the Bath estate in the 1840s was attributed to the effect of the subsidization scheme.

The great famine in County Monaghan and South Ulster had similar consequences to the famine in the north-west of Ulster. Sixty thousand people were lost as a result of the blight in a few years – more than the population decline in the provinces of Munster, Ulster or Connaught in the 1950s. In 1938, the Irish Folklore Commissioners' schools survey reported the impact of the famine. References were made to part of the Shercock–Castleblayney road that was built in 1846 by poor farmers, who had to provide their own wheelbarrows. There were references to 'porridge houses' for the distribution of oatmeal porridge in the parish of Aghnamullen. Others were mentioned that distributed government broth. On Porridge Hill in the parish of Tedavnet, Williamson's house provided gruel every second day for the paupers. There were many more such sites and places associated with the famine – relief houses, outbuildings and sheds of the workhouses. There was also the question of how the social upheaval of the 1840s had affected graves.

An examination of the social catastrophe that was the famine shows that the people who were most affected were the very poor. These were made up of cottiers and landless people – the 'broken down' and 'useless' tenants on the Shirley estate and paupers that were 'shovelled out' under the various emigration schemes. They were rejected by the authorities, which saw their disappearance as a benefit. Their troubles were mostly unnoticed by the rest of the community. They lived in hovels, many of which were destroyed when the poor had left. Travellers on the roadside disappeared into the mist of history.

Chapter 9

The Great Hunger in County Tyrone

Tyrone, according to the statistics, was the part of Ulster least affected by the famine. The potato crop partially failed in 1845, but this does not seem to have had any great effect upon the countryside. For example, no local efforts were made by the relief committees to take advantage of government assistance. The total failure of the 1846 potato crop caused more or less the same reaction, but from early October, local relief committees started to respond to local needs. There were twenty-eight committees in correspondence with Dublin Castle, but the relief measures did not begin to operate until November or December. Calls were made in various localities for the adoption of the government's principal relief measure – the public works scheme. The use of the scheme was not universal, and only four counties in Ireland recorded fever numbers. An estimated 11,500 people in County Tyrone were sustained by public works from mid-November 1846 until the end of March 1847.

An analysis of the public works in County Tyrone shows that a large sum was spent in the barony of Upper Strabane, centred on Gortin, where £7,777 was set aside for seventy-six roadworks, of which nineteen were new and the rest improvements. In East Omagh, which was a large barony running north-east to south-west from Carrickmore to Omagh to Dromore to Trillick, £4,323 was spent on ninety-three roadworks. Only twenty of these were improvements. Lower Strabane, stretching from Dunnamanagh through Strabane to Newtownstewart was allocated just under £2,500 for thirty road improvements, six new road sections and one stone-breaking scheme. The three subdivisions of the large district which occupied the east of the county, namely Upper, Middle and Lower Dungannon, were awarded £2,000. West Omagh, the smallest barony, and Clogher, centred on the town, had forty-five and twenty roadworks respectively.

Examples of roadworks from East Omagh show how far subsidies would go. Of £218 levied in the Beragh division, £142 was earmarked to build a new road from Beragh to Ballygawley, in the townlands of Clogherney and Dredargan. In the Dromore division, £35 was earmarked to cut through two hills and to fill up two hollows on the road from Dromore to Edeney; and £50 was earmarked for repairing the side streets of Dromore. There was a limit to public works in County Tyrone, and this illustrates some of the common problems in the baronies relief system. Most of the works in the county seem to have gone ahead without incident.

A report in mid-December 1846 noted that, in the barony of East Omagh, a number of gangs were engaged in some parts by the Board of Works, but they delayed putting in an appearance. Despite the destitution, works had not been started.

A meeting of the landlords and cess-payers of East Omagh was held on 13 October. This called upon the Lord Lieutenant to proclaim an extraordinary presentment session, as requested by the public works legislation. The session was held at the Omagh courthouse on 26 October, and nearly £5,000 was raised for roadworks.

The Board of Works took five weeks to present its report to the Treasury on the first batch of works, of which there were forty-four in all. It was another week before the first Treasury sanction came through, accounting for just under £2,000. By December, smaller amounts were sanctioned, but it was late in January before there was another substantial allocation – £1,700 for roadworks. It took nearly two months between a request and Treasury approval for the first of the relief payments and a further month for the remainder. This was supposed to be an emergency system of famine relief.

Works were insufficient. In the barony of Strabane it was reported that although almost all of the poor who had applied for relief received it, about 1,200 were employed. Some of the amounts provided for this work were nearly expended, making fresh presentments necessary. Clogher Relief Committee took its task seriously, providing lists of the poor for employment. Five hundred labourers were enrolled by early January 1847. The committee also believed that numbers would rise in the weeks to follow, and that they could be employed. Fintona had similar problems, made worse by the late start to the works. In February, Charles Eccles, the chairman, said that the list of labourers contained up to 700 names, but only about 160 were employed. The area contained a population of 12,000, of whom at least one third did not have a single day's food in reserve. Fever, dysentery and diarrhoea prevailed to an alarming extent amongst the poor. At about the same time, employment on public works around Omagh was gradually falling. The workhouse, which was built to house 800 poor, contained 1,200. Most of these people had been hurriedly admitted. They were not as yet provided with clothing of any kind, and most had only the clothes they stood up in.

Wages were poor, due to two principal factors: first, government policy required wages to be twopence per day (less than the local rate); secondly, there was a steep increase in the cost of food. Clogher Relief Committee had to supply reduced-price meals to labourers on the works who had large families. Half of the 500 employed required this help.

Urney Relief Committee distributed food tickets every Saturday to these unfortunate labourers. Officialdom disapproved and threatened to withhold substantial aid from the committee's fund. The Board of Works inspecting officers from Tyrone, led by Captain Oldershaw, reported visiting a quarry near Strabane where the labourers complained that the stone they were breaking was so hard that they were unable to earn a day's wages at the price fixed. Captain Oldershaw agreed that the stone was uncommonly hard and he asked the authorities to allow the men something extra.

Similar problems were also experienced by Oldershaw's colleague, Lieutenant Columb. It was stony ground and there were a lot of large hard stones in the drainage area. It was impossible for the men to earn enough to support themselves at the rate of four pence per perch.

One of the most serious problems, and a source of disagreement amongst the landholders was deciding what action to take to relieve distress. Many landlords worried about the public works scheme, especially after the government's insistence that the work was unproductive. Another anxiety was the compulsory nature of the extraordinary presentment session, which followed the Lord Lieutenant's declaration of a 'poor' area. The concern was that such sessions could be inundated by large crowds – which had occurred already in a few sessions in County Cavan and County Monaghan.

The sessions in County Tyrone did not avoid the excitement which took place at such meetings all over the county. At Clogher, on 12 October 1846, the galleries were filled to capacity, but the people were well behaved. In the barony of Strabane, on 16 October, the attendance was great, and the room crowded to excess. At Strabane, on the following day, the ratepayers and the labouring class were very numerous, and the galleries and main body of the court were densely crowded. The situation was mirrored at Castlederg a few days later. The exception was the Lower Dungannon session at Aughnacloy on 4 November, which was poorly attended. There was only one magistrate present and the proceedings were delayed for an hour before the meeting was begun.

At Clogher, the atmosphere was volatile. The crowd regarded the results of the approaching proceedings as crucial. At first there was agreement that the barony should opt for drainage works. The roll call of electoral divisions represented showed that many of them wanted some sort of roadworks as well as drainage systems. The meeting was adjourned and it was agreed that the Reverend Duogh, PP should speak on behalf of the starving people before work commenced. He said that people were starving in the town of Augher, and throughout the county. Many were living solely on cabbage. At this, there were cheers and shouts of "Relief for Ireland" from the gallery and the meeting adjourned.

A session held at Cookstown on 2 November for the barony of Upper Dungannon was quite uncontrolled. The weather was favourable and a vast multitude assembled outside. There was a rush into the courthouse when the doors were opened. The chairman was cheered when he announced that, despite the objections echoed at several Tyrone sessions, care for the poor would still be a priority. The public became impatient with discussions amongst magnates, at one stage shouting that they wanted some person to speak for them, otherwise their wants and wishes would not be attended to. Their temper was aroused some time later by a cess-payer from Drumancey who thought that there was not much destitution in his part of the county. They reacted strongly to this observation and disrupted the proceedings for a considerable period.

A spokesman for the Dublin, Belfast & Coleraine Junction Railway started to speak, but he was confronted by the most desperate cries of protest from the multitudes.

Colonel Stuart brought the meeting to an end and asked all to disperse quickly. The crowd would not comply, and several of them said that they would keep the magistrates informed of what was happening. There seemed to be no passage to the door except over the heads of the crowd, but several members of the session forced their way through. One gentleman was pushed on the stairs and he called the policeman to make an arrest. This was the signal for general rioting, and the local press condemned it as a 'scene of insanity'. The labouring classes were up in arms and informed the visitors of their starvation level.

Arrangements for the barony of Middle Dungannon provide a good illustration of the position of the landlords. They had a session of discourses about whether to ask the Lord Lieutenant for an extraordinary session. At their final meeting in late October, Lord Northland, on behalf of himself and his father, Lord Ranfurly, who were the proprietors of the land of Dungannon, objected to an extraordinary session (i.e. to the use of public works of the town of Dungannon). They proposed instead to take charge of and secure the poor on their estate – tenants and cottiers – so that no one living on the property should want. Lord Northland further proposed, on behalf of his father, a private subscription of £5 per week to be distributed amongst the poor. One condition was that the lands should be administered by his agent, who would take care of donations. Lord Northland called upon other landlords to take similar action, but they asked him to withdraw his objection to public works. A few days later, extraordinary sessions were announced for Upper Dungannon at Cookstown on 2 November, and at Aughnacloy on 4 November.

All of the works decided upon in Upper and Middle Dungannon were modelled on those in Lower Dungannon, where there were successful drainage works. These public works were a notable concession wrought from the government by a sustained campaign supported by the wealthy landlords of every party. Ireland as a whole only contributed five per cent of the monies expended on public works schemes. The main requirement was that each individual proprietor granting the concession had to give an undertaking that funds paid out should be used exclusively on the lands to be improved. This deterred many landlords who were eager for access to public funds. Public works were for drainage – a worthwhile enterprise. The landlords of the barony of Dungannon showed some degree of determination – a rare commodity amongst landlords where money was involved. The arrangements of Labouchere's letter, although aimed at the land, were not good for out-of-work labourers and small farmers. The arrangements were shown to have an effect on the public works. Landlords were tight as far as paying out money was concerned, especially when they were unsure of the outcome.

Henry Lowry-Corry, MP, wrote to his agent on his realization of the extent of the 1846 potato failure. He said that there was no limit to the help that he might provide. The people would not be allowed to starve if he could help.

Most people in County Tyrone wanted to engage in 'Labouchere's drainage', but on two occasions they failed to do so – at Clogher and West Omagh there was a lack of agreement. At least one session appears to have taken the advice of the MP, Sir R. H. Ferguson. Roadworks were opted for, for the barony required them.

Public works in County Tyrone seem to have been of a very high standard, and this gave satisfaction to the Board of Works, who supervised them and provided inspecting officers. Captain Oldershaw reported that between mid-November 1846 and the end of February 1847 the works in general were proceeding satisfactorily. The county was quiet and the people at peace. He acknowledged that such good order was maintained in spite of great difficulties. He said that there was a large number of destitute poor in the county, but that there were no reports of misconduct. The county, he said, although in a sorry state of destitution, was perfectly quiet. People worked well and very hard and those chosen from amongst them were loyal. He also mentioned the role of the relief committees in providing work for the destitute. They boasted that the public works were managed well in the rural areas. Business was conducted impartially, and Oldershaw was the only person of importance in Ulster who spoke so well about local committees.

The winter was severe. A glimpse of conditions was given in the officers' memorandum about the winter of 1846/7. On top of the trauma of the total failure of the potato crop, the people had to endure the first wild winter for years, as a contemporary expressed it. In late November it was reported that in the neighbourhood of Omagh the snow was falling thick, and the winds blew stormy until daybreak. The gangs knocked off work, but the houses remained damp – here there was perhaps a hope of obtaining lucrative work. The snow was falling, and was generally about six inches deep, though in other places much more. In January, heavy rain caused havoc and new monies had to be raised. In early February, heavy snow and frost interrupted both farming and drainage work.

The food shortage in County Tyrone was starting to bite.

In general the works undertaken in County Tyrone were very typical of schemes in Ireland. There were rural improvements – 183 altogether – and ninety-four new sections. Tyrone was typical in having a large number of drainage works – forty-three altogether, or 27.5 per cent of all the public works in the county. As well as roadworks and drainage schemes there were two attempts to secure canal and railway undertakings as public works. A £30,000 outlay was proposed for a ship canal running from Strabane to the Foyle on condition that the landlord, the Marquess of Abercorn, should share responsibility for the scheme. It would make a rent charge on his estate. These stipulations seem to fit the Labouchere conditions. A maximum of £40,000 was donated for the earthworks and masonry, etc. for that portion of the Londonderry & Enniskillen and Londonderry & Coleraine railway companies. The petition stated that railway construction would prevent many labourers from being thrown on the public works. Each line was highlighted, but the need for the Enniskillen line was by far the most urgent. The petition also stated that the railway construction would provide much work for the county, and easy access to Londonderry, the port of departure to England and Scotland. A similar attempt was made at this session for Upper Dungannon on behalf of the Dublin, Belfast & Coleraine Junction Railway. After careful consideration, the government decided that loans to the railway company were not the way to relieve distress. This was a way of saying that it was not sympathetic to private companies joining forces with baronial sessions to make use of public funds.

After the total failure of the potato crop in 1846 many relief committees started to form – a sure sign that the leadership of local committees perceived a great need of help among those who were reliant upon the potato as their staple diet. The chairman of the Clogher Relief Committee wrote in October 1846 that the farms in the neighbourhood were generally very small, and that the persons holding them with their families depended almost entirely upon the potato. The formation of the relief committee did not depend solely on local leadership. As a result of previous famines, the mechanization of government-supported local efforts had been set up in 1845 and were well established. In early October 1846 all county lieutenants were ordered by the government's Relief Commission in Dublin to divide the counties into relief districts. The Tyrone county lieutenant, the Earl of Charlemont, nominated a series of appointments at the end of October. With the exception of four (for which no records survive) the committees in order of Charlemont's appointments were: Cookstown, Gortin, Omagh, Castlederg, Trillick, Stewartstown, Fivemiletown, Fintona, Newtownstewart, Caledon, Moy, Aughnacloy, Dungannon and Leckpatrick.

Using the correspondence of local committees as a guide, it is possible to ascertain the chronology of their operation. The Aughnacloy and Clogher committees seem to have been the first into action, around October.

In early November, most of the townlands were starting to function. There was no further communication between the Augher, Fivemiletown and Cookstown committees and the Relief Commission.

There appears to be a degree of confusion in the appointment of the local committees; but this only reflects reality. There was a great deal of uniformity of response, due mainly to the government's 'Instructions' for the formation of local committees, published on 8 October 1846. There was a considerable degree of duplicated activity. The rector of the parish of Desertcreat appealed for government aid, and he has left an account of prevailing conditions. The landlords were spread over various parishes, and as a result there was no concerted plan. Several funds were managed by the local relief committees. Meal was given weekly to the poor. Letters were written describing conditions. Various subscriptions were raised that were rubber-stamped by the lieutenant of the county but they were ineligible for a grant. The exception was Cookstown, whose committee covered the petty sessions district, but whose activities were limited. The Cookstown committee was not prepared for external relief. There is no one concerted plan of relief, and the requirements of the landlords took precedence over the needs of the poor. However, they considered the destitute on their property as their problem. To bring the government into the situation was perhaps an invitation to subsequent taxation. However, efforts were made to bring the poor under the care of the authorities.

A local confusion is provided by the parish committee of the curacy of Moy, which was between the Moy and Dungannon relief districts. The curate, the Reverend John Leach, was treasurer of the Moy committee, which did not establish a soup kitchen, but the curate established one with a small parochial fund, and this was much appreciated in the neighbourhood. It distributed about ninety quarts each day of the week, Sunday excepted. His request for grant aid to his fund was granted. On the other hand, part of the curacy lay within the Dungannon relief district. The subcommittees of Dungannon embraced the parish of Killyman, whose fund was guaranteed. The Reverend Leach pleaded along similar lines. There were two aspects of organization and outlook which distinguished relief committees in County Tyrone from those in other parts of the province. The difference in organization was widespread in the county relief districts, based upon petty-sessions districts. There were differences in outlook, and it was held that the committees sold food at reasonable prices.

In the appointment of local committees and the delineation of relief districts the county lieutenant was given a free hand. The 'Instructions' of October 1846 favoured smaller districts (including two parishes), though there were larger central committees. Funds were granted if the county lieutenant found it desirable. The lieutenants followed their own preferences. The central committees were extensively used by the

Earl of Erne in Fermanagh and by John Young, MP, acting lieutenant for County Cavan. In Donegal, Vice-Lieutenant Sir James Stewart adhered to two parish districts. In County Londonderry, Sir Robert Ferguson preferred to use electoral divisions of Poor Law Unions. The strong preference of Lord Chartemore in County Tyrone was for four petty-sessions districts. All these districts in the barony of Clogher (Clogher, Ballygawley and Fintona) were petty-sessions districts. So too were Omagh and Carrickmore in the barony of East Omagh. At Cookstown in Upper Dungannon and Aughnacloy in Lower Dungannon attempts were made to use central committees. Dungannon Relief Committee embraced the parishes of Drumglass, Donaghamore and Killyman, with the district of Castlecaulfield/Edencrannon. Stewartstown had subcommittees at Arboe, Clonloe and Ballyclog. In the barony of Lower Strabane, all the districts were parochial, advocating moderation, but it was a serious administrative liability when, at the turn of 1846/7, the government lost faith in local bodies. The Temporary Relief Act expanded the Poor Law system to help those affected by the famine. There was chaos and confusion as the Poor Law electoral divisions were forced upon the paupers. It was popularly known as the Soup Kitchen Act or Rations Act. It was financed out of the poor rate, and administered by the local relief committees, which were reorganized on a uniform system.

Local relief committees were expected to provide food, and lists of applicants were scrutinized for employment for public works. Supplies of Indian corn were expected to be provided. Finance came from locally raised relief funds, but there was also support through government assistance. Up to mid-January 1847 the grant was usually fifty per cent, and thereafter it was usually one hundred per cent. The 'Instructions' were quite specific that committees should sell food, although in small quantities, and only to persons who were known to them. The price they charged should be the same as the market price which obtained in the area. When the workhouses were full, committees had to provide extensive assistance to persons not capable of taking up labour of any kind.

There is evidence that there was widespread opposition to government policy. In Ulster the most serious critics were rewarded. Tyrone committees – namely, Moy and Dunnamanagh – made no secret of their breach of the famine conditions; they demanded government aid. Moy Relief Committee anticipated at the start of November 1846 that it would have to provide money and funds for a large number of the poor. From infancy to old age they had little prospect of work. The Dungannon Union workhouses, including the Moy workhouse, were overflowing. The committee was also supplying meals to poor families at a reduced price. James Eyre Jackson admitted that it was not in accord with the 'Instructions'. He argued that the committee was unable to devise any other means that were not equally or more objectionable.

Many schemes for providing employment were considered, but they were more expensive than the plans to sell meal at a penny a pound. Those holding at least four acres were refused relief by the committee. When these admissions were made, the situation had deteriorated. On these grounds, Jackson pressed for a government donation towards their fund of £315, of which £120 had been spent by that November. He presented a circular of 20 January in which he set out his policy on the issues and on the sale of food. Where food was provided, cost had to be taken into account. If the committee consented, a donation would be recommended.

Jackson stated that his committee was of the opinion that their system had worked well. He further stated that the poor would appreciate aid. This principle, he said, was recognized by Routh himself. The government grants ceased to be insufficient, but they were, of course, augmented by the private subscriptions. The committee wanted to help the destitute by giving the moral support that buying at a penny a pound would give. The committee was fully aware that the main object was 'sale at first cost'. They tried not to fight off the private supplying of food. In the Moy district, this did not apply, for it was not retail traders that were lacking but the supply of money to buy food.

Henry Colthurst, secretary to the Dunnamanagh committee, assured his colleagues about the position on the land – for example, regarding the difficulty of bringing about the needed food sales in the district. The committee gave relief to the destitute, as the 'Instructions' permitted (i.e. the Relief Commission and the Poor Law), and this was designed for different classes of recipients. The position of the committees was well understood: affording relief under the Poor Law, especially in the south and west of Ireland, where destitution was most severe. If the committee were to sell meal only at first cost, as the 'Instructions' required, the whole amount of the relief fund would remain in good order. Absolute paupers were taken care of in the workhouse. The committee directed that the money should be spent in Poor Law relief. Well-to-do families were requested to make contributions. Parents were productively employed, but, due to the combined operation of low wages and high prices, they were unable to earn enough to support their families. The usual practice in the area was for the farmer to employ his cottiers or labourers two or five days in the week, but they needed to find other work to earn enough to live.

Another large class in the area were the weavers, who were only employed part-time due to the depression in the linen business. Labourers and weavers could now earn ten pence per day, even if fully employed. Meal was sold at twopence per pound. The average family had one meal a day.

At length, the committee was anxious to impress upon Routh that charity was not open-ended. They sold a week's supply (10lb) of Indian meal at the reduced price of one shilling. They did not have an unlimited quantity, but they now permitted their applicants to possess a whole week's supply at a reduced price. The allowance was 2lb per week for each member of the family, and it was only available to those families that were in dire straits and where it was proven to the committee that they had neither cows, corn or any other means of support. The committee boasted that they had the working man's plight at heart – there were the profits of the retail trader to be taken into account! What transpired was that the recipients avoided starvation. The secretary said he had full confidence in the committee, and he assured Routh that they would judge each case on its merits.

As well as the Moy and Dunnamanagh committees there were several other committees in County Tyrone that admitted openly to selling meal at reduced prices. From the beginning of the operation in early November, Dungannon noted special prices in regard to the sale of food – otherwise the poor lived without subscriptions. At Newtownstewart, there were three depots for selling meal at a reduced price. Meal was sold at one shilling per peck, in varying quantities, from half a peck to two pecks, according to the number of people in the individual families and the extent of destitution. Clogher had a similar system for selling meal at a reduced price. At Pomeroy, meal was sold at one shilling and one penny per pound.

Some committees, such as Clonloe, wanted to demonstrate their efforts in following government guidelines, and they claimed to provide relief in such a way as not to interfere with the current market prices of provisions. Tickets were issued to three retailers for meal in different parts of the district. The committee paid one moiety and purchased the other. It was similar to an earlier scheme at East Urney that assisted three destitute labourers on public works whose families were so large that their weakly earnings could not provide them with food sufficient to sustain them. On Saturday nights the committee issued tickets for so many pecks of meal, which would compete at the shops in every part of the district. Payment was made to the merchants. The scheme, as far as the committee was concerned, would not only not injure the 'fair trader' but would be a decided advantage to him. Routh rejected the scheme, and he told the committee that it involved the adoption of the Aid-of-Wages system, which provided much meal in Ireland under the late Poor Law. This was a reference to the earlier Poor Law, which had been superseded by 1834. For this reason, Routh was given permission to authorize a government donation to the Urney Relief Fund. However, he did not hesitate in providing relief to Clonloe. This difference of treatment can be explained by the timing of two applications at the beginning of December and the beginning of January. Between the two dates the situation in Ireland had worsened. The result was that the application of government policy was relaxed. In January the government decided to increase grant aid on the donations to the committee from fifty per cent to one hundred per cent. East Urney also received grant aid, like other rule-breaking committees. There was also dialogue between the county and Dublin Castle, and this reflects the destitute nature of the countryside in the years 1846–7. One of the earliest warnings came from the parish of Urney in early November 1846. It said that the people were almost in despair. Hunger, like necessity, has no laws. Later, in Strabane, the famine affected 340 families (or about 1,800 people), and they were listed for relief. By early February, the fate of these people had become awful.

In the New Year, many committees echoed the observations of the Reverend Robert Maude, Dean of Clogher. He said that the cycle of destitution was rapidly gaining momentum and extending to the upper classes of the agricultural population. The Aughnacloy committee pleaded that their fund was too little. Similar complaints were heard at Coalisland, where the funds were insufficient to meet daily needs. In nearby Clonloe the distress was beyond description and the majority of people were in a state of great destitution and starvation. The Moy committee chairman stated that there was great and general destitution in his district. Linen manufacture was depressed and the farmers had dismissed their servants.

Around Pomeroy there was much suffering. Every day presented fresh scenes of horror and misery, and there was no aid available. As far as the Leckpatrick committee secretary was concerned, starvation was at its doors and it was hitting the labouring classes most severely. The universal cry was that wives and children were dying of hunger. Around Dunnamanagh, destitution and sickness prevailed in the whole district to a great degree. One of the most poignant consequences of the distress was described by the Reverend Henry Lucas St George, Rector of

Dromore, who in the middle of March said that many had died of want. However, there was some exaggeration. Many of the reports came from begging letters, seeking government help from diminishing or inadequate funds, but the overall situation was that the poor were in too serious a condition for the plight to be ignored.

The use of the Temporary Relief Act provides us with useful information about the extent of the famine in different parts of County Tyrone. A full range of statistics for the generation of the Act between April and August 1847 had been compiled. Since the Act was administered, the Poor Law system was implemented in an attempt to keep starvation at bay within each electoral division in the unions.

The most immediately useful result is encapsulated by the maxim that relief should be administered daily to all those in need. It was expressed as a percentage of the population of the union or electoral division as a fact of the 1841 census. The poor in the Omagh and Clogher unions were relieved by the committees at Strabane, Castlederg, Dungannon, Cookstown and Gortin. A close look shows that numerous electoral divisions in the Strabane Union were badly off in comparison with those in other unions. The Moyle division of the Gortin Union had 35.4 per cent of its population recovering, as against a union average of 9.24 per cent. In the Castlederg Union the average figure was 16.22 per cent. The West Drumquin division had 25.64 per cent on rations.

There were stress points within the Poor Law Unions of County Tyrone, arranged in descending order of percentage of the population receiving food. Another difference shown by the statistics for the Temporary Relief Act is the method by which different funds were raised. Two of the larger ones were loans under the individual electoral divisions by the government. Further land subscriptions were raised, on top of which the government continued to give donations. There was a multiplicity of landlords, a considerable degree of absenteeism and a lack of agreement about what measures should be taken. In more prosperous areas, where the economy was strong and where there was leadership, they tended to provide for themselves by further local subscriptions. Prosperous areas had the benefit of one hundred per cent government support, whilst the least prosperous areas were burdened with the debt of the full amount of the government loan.

There were serious pressures in the workhouses in the autumn of 1846. The blight was spreading during the first six or seven days of August. In one union, where potatoes were grown on workhouse land, the board of guardians refused to use the crop before it became diseased. In Clogher, where the potatoes had only been planted in May, the guardians ordered 5lb of potatoes to be given daily to each inmate instead of meal so long as the famine lasted. The potato crop, totalling 760 stones, was eaten during three weeks in August.

The influx into the workhouses increased all over Ireland in October 1846. By this time of the year, twenty-one out of fifty-three workhouses were filled to more than their capacity. The poor fare at the Tyrone workhouse was recorded. As the workhouses began to fill up, all kinds of temporary relief was used to help with accommodation. Alternatively, wooden sheds in the workhouse grounds were used as accommodation. By the beginning of February, the Omagh workhouse was very overcrowded. The medical officer distributed shirts to nearly all the occupants, including the children. However, the disease was starting to take its grip upon events. The sick were lying close together, but an epidemic did not materialize. Temporary hospitals were arranged in the Omagh, Fintona and Dromore divisions in the first half of July. One small hospital, with provision for twenty patients, was established at Pomeroy and another in Cookstown. The winter of 1846/7 was severe, and extreme distress and suffering were experienced by the poor.

Afterword

The history of the famine in Ulster is a tale of misery and sickness, in keeping with the situation in the rest of Ireland. It is significant that the people of Ulster today – mostly Protestants – do not blame the policies of the British Government for the blight on the potatoes. By the beginning of 1850 the blight had taken its course, and the land once again yielded a good crop of potatoes. Today, in Ulster, potatoes are a favourite dish, and there is little prospect that the conditions of the mid-nineteenth century in Ireland will ever be repeated.

Select Bibliography

Alexander Somerville, *Letters from Ireland during the Famine of 1847* (Irish Academic Press, 1994)

Anthony Trollope, *The Irish Famine* (Silverbridge Press, 1987)

Cathal Póirtéir (ed.), *The Great Irish Famine* (Mercier Press, 1995)

Cathal Póirtéir (ed.), *Famine Echoes* (Gill & Macmillan, 1995)

Cecil Woodham-Smith, *The Great Hunger* (Hamish Hamilton, 1962)

Christine Kinealy, *This Great Calamity* (Gill & Macmillan, 1994)

Christine Kinealy, *The Hidden Famine* (Pluto Press, 2000)

Christine Kinealy and Trevor Parkhill (ed.), *The Famine in Ulster* (Ulster Historical Foundation, 1997)

Cormar Ó Gráda, *The Great Irish Famine* (Cambridge University Press, 1995)

David Dickson, *Arctic Ireland* (The White Row Press, 1997)

David Fitzpatrick, *Irish Emigration, 1801–1921* (Dundalgan Press, 1984)

Kieran A. Kennedy, *From Famine to Feast* (Institute of Public Administration, 1998)

John O'Rourke, *The Great Irish Famine* (Veritas, 1989)

Maldwyn A. Jones, *Destination America* (Fontana/Collins, 1996)

Margaret Crawford (ed.), *The Hungry Stream* (Institute of Irish Studies, 1997)

Mary E. Daly, *The Famine in Ireland* (Dundalgan Press, 1986)

Robert James Scally, *The End of Hidden Ireland* (Oxford University Press, 1995)

Robert Whyte, *1847 Famine Ship Diary* (Mercier Press, 1994)